AUTHOR

Salvo Fagone was born in Catania in 1979, the city where he graduated in Computer Science at the University of Catania. He has always been a scholar of ancient and modern history, and in 2016 he began a collaboration with the DPAA, an institution of the U.S. Department of Defense that deals with the search for soldiers missing in war. During the years he has conducted research at the archives of the AFHRA, at Maxwell AFB, in Alabama, at the NARA in Washington DC, in the United States of America, and also in Canada, at the Library and Archives Canada (LAC), in England, at The National Archives (TNA) in Kew, in the French archives Le Service Historique de l'Armée de l'Air (SHAA), in the German Bundesarchiv and in the New Zealand archives of Auckland. He has written articles for various national and international periodicals. In October 2019, he published his first work, entitled "Reconnaissance on Huskies. The Crucial Role of Air Reconnaissance and Ultra Intelligence over Sicily and the Mediterranean. 1940-1943".

PUBLISHING'S NOTES

None of unpublished images or text of our book may be reproduced in any format without the expressed written permission of Luca Cristini Editore (already Soldiershop.com) when not indicate as marked with license creative commons 3.0 or 4.0. Luca Cristini Editore has made every reasonable effort to locate, contact and acknowledge rights holders and to correctly apply terms and conditions to Content.

Every effort has been made to trace the copyright of all the photographs. If there are unintentional omissions, please contact the publisher in writing at: info@soldiershop.com, who will correct all subsequent editions.

Our trademark: Luca Cristini Editore©, and the names of our series & brand: Soldiershop, Witness to war, Museum book, Bookmoon, Soldiers&Weapons, Battlefield, War in colour, Historical Biographies, Darwin's view, Fabula, Altrastoria, Italia Storica Ebook, Witness To History, Soldiers, Weapons & Uniforms, Storia etc. are herein © by Luca Cristini Editore.

LICENSES COMMONS

This book may utilize part of material marked with license creative commons 3.0 or 4.0 (CC BY 4.0), (CC BY-ND 4.0), (CC BY-SA 4.0) or (CC0 1.0). We give appropriate attribution credit and indicate if change were made in the acknowledgments field. Our WTW books series utilize only fonts licensed under the SIL Open Font License or other free use license.

For a complete list of Soldiershop titles please contact Luca Cristini Editore on our website: www.soldiershop.com or www.cristinieditore.com. E-mail: info@soldiershop.com

On cover : A SAAF Baltimore probably stuck in the Capodichino airport in Naples. Ground and flight personnel without the aid of mechanical means pull the aircraft out of the quagmire.
Small image: The badge of the 55 Squadron with the motto "NIL NOS TREME FACIT".

Title: **ROAD TO ROME** Code.: **WTW-026 ENG** By Salvo Fagone
ISBN code: 978-88-93277730 First edition July 2021
English text Nr. of images:112 Layout: 177,8x254mm Cover & Art Design: Luca S. Cristini

WITNESS TO WAR (SOLDIERSHOP) is a trademark of Luca Cristini Editore, via Orio, 35/4 - 24050 Zanica (BG) ITALY.

WITNESS TO WAR

ROAD TO ROME

SHOTS AND MEMORIES OF A RHODESIAN IN THE RAF

PHOTOS & IMAGES FROM WORLD WARTIME ARCHIVES

SALVO FAGONE

BOOKS TO COLLECT

CONTENTS

Introduction..5

Algernon de Blois Spurr..6

The Casablanca Conference..7

Operation Corkscrew..8

Operation Husky...10

The retreat from Sicily..35

Rome is bombed...37

July, 19th 1943..37

August, 13th 1943..40

Italy surrenders...41

The war continues...57

Target: Roma..58

Brief history of the 55 Squadron RAF..87

Bibliography...97

INTRODUCTION

Normally, in World War II literature, most contemporary authors have focused their attention on the great war operations, the Aces of aerial fighters or the great protagonists, winners or losers, of famous battles.

My purpose is, instead, to tell the photographic story of a simple airman, who never held a weapon or any sort of offensive means against the enemy, but only a small Zeiss Super Ikonta 530/16 camera for personal use and a Williamson F.24 aerial camera in use by the departments.

It is indeed a great pleasure and honor for me to dedicate this short historical essay to the father of my friend Brian Spurr. My connection with the history of Algernon de Blois Spurr began by chance, when years ago I was busy writing my first work, Reconnaissance on Husky. Writing a historical essay presupposes a long process of research and documentation; and it was during this delicate and challenging phase that I met Brian, a South African reporter, who told me about his father, a war photographer during the Second World War. Algy, as he was known to his friends, had been assigned to an air reconnaissance unit in the Mediterranean area, and had later joined the 55 Squadron RAF, belonging to the 232 Wing of the Royal Air Force in the Italian Campaign.

When Brian pulled out the photographs his father had taken during the war from his drawer of memories, I was totally fascinated. Brian was young when his father died. The pictures taken by Algernon are numerous, and they cover a vast chronological period; they follow the war operations of the unit from behind the front lines and its movements from one end of Italy to the other, in a journey that took him from North Africa to Rome. His shots alternated scenes of war with everyday life scenes, portraying in an impromptu way the ordinary people he met by chance on the street.

Although Algernon de Blois Spurr has left us a valuable photographic collection, his untimely death, at only 40 years old, has unfortunately, not given us the opportunity to collect, his memoirs. I therefore decided to use his pictures to follow his journey around Italy, following in the footsteps of the 55 Squadron RAF and the events of the war that characterized those years. Many of the photos, still in negative, were later developed by his son, who inherited from his father the passion for photography, becoming a professional photographer. In some cases, it was not even possible to identify with certainty the places portrayed, but it was decided to include them anyway, thus leaving the reader the possibility to assume and travel with the mind, in time and space, and to accompany Algernon in his last long journey to the Eternal City.

I thank, therefore, Brian Spurr, for the privilege, so generously granted to me, hoping to give the proper credit to the memory of his father.

The author

ALGERNON DE BLOIS SPURR

My father, Algernon de Blois Spurr, was born on May 21, 1920 in Salisbury (now Harare), Rhodesia (now Zimbabwe). He attended school at Milton High School in Bulawayo. On March 19, 1940, he enlisted in the Southern Rhodesian Air Force at Belvedere in Salisbury. He transferred to the Royal Air Force in October 1940 (service number SR777997). By the end of the year, he was stationed at Cranborne Air Station in Salisbury.

On the last day of 1940, he was in a group leaving for the Middle East. They left by train and went to Durban, South Africa. There he boarded a ship bound for Mombasa and then ended up inland in Nairobi for three months. He was then assigned as a photographer; he wanted to become a pilot, but it turned out he was color blind. Leaving Mombasa by ship, he went via Port Sudan to Port Said. At that time, he was in the staff of No.2 PRU (Photographic Reconnaissance Unit). From March 1941 to September 1942, the unit was based at Heliopolis, just outside Cairo, Egypt. They were equipped with Spitfires, Beaufighters and Mosquitoes. On February 1, 1942, he was reclassified as LAC (Leading Aircraftman - Photographer). From September to December 1942, he moved with the unit to Lebanon (Beirut) and Syria. From the end of December 1942 until January 1943 he returned to Egypt, to Kilo 8 (an airstrip near the Tunisian border). He joined 232 Wing RAF and from February to April 1943 he was at El Daba LG106.

Here he was posted to the 55 Squadron RAF as they moved westward along North Africa, through Libya (Tripoli) and Tunisia (Tunis). In August 1943 they went by ship to Sicily and remained there until mid-September 1943. He went through the plain of Catania, which allowed him to take some pictures of Mount Etna. Among the places he passed through were Licata, Gela, Syracuse, and Messina. Then he passed through the peninsula and, it is unclear, but it seems he returned to North Africa and then back to Italy again, where he passed through places like Foggia, Villa San Giovanni, photographed Vesuvius (photos in eruption of March/April 1944), and then again Campo Marino, Rome, Pisa, Cecina, to name a few.

In December 1944 he returned to Cairo, and at the end of the year he returned to Rhodesia. In September 1945 he was discharged from the Air Force and enlisted in the civil service as a customs officer. He was 25 years old. He married my mother in 1947 and had two children, my brother and me. Unfortunately, he died of tuberculosis at the age of 40, which is why his story is a little difficult for me to tell as I was too young to ask him about his experiences. We believe that he contracted tuberculosis in Egypt during the war and then failed to get treatment in due time.

My father's wartime service was in many ways a good experience since he was usually located far behind his own lines. His job was to mount the cameras onto the aircraft ready for sorties and to process and analyze the images. The photographers were able to see many places, enjoy some time in Cairo and on the beaches of the Mediterranean. They had a trailer that served as a facility for photographic developing and processing. Conditions, however, were tough in the desert, with the heat and sand. They also dug trenches and lived spaced apart from each other to limit damage in the event of an enemy attack.

When he passed away, I was only eleven years old. I still miss him to this day....

In memory of my father.
Brian Spurr (his son)

THE CASABLANCA CONFERENCE

The British victory obtained at El Alamein on November 4, 1942 had entailed strategic results that went far beyond its immediate consequences. Among them, the first major defeat suffered by German General Erwin Rommel, the only German superior commander to foresee the long-term implications of El Alamein, deserves a prominent place. For this very reason, Generalfeldmarschall had long insisted that Hitler withdraw German forces from North Africa while there was still time. The Desert Fox met Hitler at the Führer's headquarters near Rastenburg, in the middle of the East Prussian forest. In his long speech, he told him that there was no hope of victory and that abandoning the African theater of war had to be considered as a real long-term political strategy.

Operation Torch, the Anglo-American invasion of Morocco and Algeria on November 8, 1942, further sealed the fate of the Axis forces in North Africa. While General Bernard Law Montgomery pursued Rommel's Army that was retreating towards Tripoli, the Allied Task Force commanded by General Dwight D. Eisenhower moved to Tunisia, where the two sides would fight to the death during the first months of 1943.

It was very clear to the German and Italian high commands that, given the massive air, naval and land forces the Allies had at their disposal, they would immediately strike in some other area of the Mediterranean once the Tunisian Campaign was over. General George C. Marshall, the architect of American strategy, who strongly disagreed with the British Prime Minister, Sir Winston Churchill, advocated direct action against Germany by means of a cross-Channel invasion of France in 1943. When the British Prime Minister and the President of the United States of America, Franklin Delano Roosevelt, met in Casablanca, a deep uncertainty reigned over the summit as to what strategy the Allies should adopt in a future war scenario and what the results would be. After strong contrasts between the British Chiefs of Staff on one side and the Americans on the other, a compromise was finally reached. The United States of America met the British demands to face further military operations in the Mediterranean, but in exchange for a renewed plan of action for the inevitable operation of the crossing of the Channel, which would soon be baptized with the name of Operation Overlord. The decision taken in Casablanca to invade Sicily, consecrated Eisenhower as Allied commander in chief for Operation Husky. General Harold Alexander was designated deputy commander in chief and commander of the ground forces. The command of all Allied naval forces fell instead to the famous Sir Andrew Browne Cunningham, commander in chief of the British Navy in the Mediterranean. For the air force the position of commander in chief of the Allied air forces in the Mediterranean was assigned to Air Marshal Sir Arthur Tedder.

The first week of May 1943 saw the final Allied rush of the African Campaign. On the 1st, 4th and 6th the B-24 Liberators of the 9th USAAF Air Force attacked Reggio Calabria (on the 4th also Taranto) and, during the night, several Sicilian towns. In total contrast to the facts, on 5 May, Benito Mussolini had given full rein to the drums in announcing the "supreme certainty of victory", receiving, as the "Corriere della Sera" headlined, "the cry of faith and dedication of the multitude", in what is defined as "the grandiose gathering in Piazza Venezia[1]".

On May 17, on a Monday, the night bombers of the RAF, the Vickers Wellingtons, left from Malta and went as far as the Lido of Rome, attacking the base of the seaplanes and launching propaganda leaflets on the city. The Allies wanted to demonstrate that the eternal city was not inviolable, and it was at their discretion to bomb it or not.

---

1 Marco Patricelli, *L'Italia sotto le bombe*, Editori Laterza, 2007, p. 165.

OPERATION CORKSCREW

When the remaining Axis forces in Tunisia surrendered on May 13, 1943, the Allied powers prepared to attack the "soft underbelly of Fortress Europe," following the vivid expression of the British Prime Minister, Sir Winston Churchill.

On the map of the central Mediterranean, there are a few remote islands that suddenly interrupt the uniformity of the blue Mediterranean Sea. The two islands of Lampedusa and Pantelleria are the most distant Italian outposts, closest to Africa and sentinels of the great mother island. For this reason, it was mandatory to conquer them first.

All Allied air power was therefore focused on the smaller islands of Sicily. Thus began the preparatory phase of Operation Corkscrew, which culminated with the occupation of the island of Pantelleria.

Already on May 9, in the preparatory phase, General Eisenhower had decided to employ on Sicily the heavy bombers of the Northwest African Strategic Air Force (NASAF) and the fighters and fighter-bombers of the Northwest African Tactical Air Force (NATAF). The Royal Air Force's Malta Air Force was to provide indirect support to the operations by escorting the bombers bound to attack the Sicilian air bases. The commander of the strategic air forces in the Mediterranean, General James H. Doolittle, who had become very popular for his daring air raid on Tokyo in April 1942, completed his preparations by deploying most of the available air forces to the area of Constantine, Souk-El-Arba and Djedeida.

The commander of the tactical air forces, Air Vice Marshal Arthur Coningham, had instead moved medium and light bombers to the fields of the Cape Bon peninsula. In total, at the beginning of the operation against Pantelleria, NATAF and NASAF together deployed 1,017 aircraft in full combat efficiency, backed up by a fair number of reserve aircraft. Given the reduced range of its numerous single-engine tactical support aircraft, the XII Air Support Command, hierarchically subordinate to NATAF, between May 20 and June 4, decentralized its units on the fields of the peninsula of Capo Bon closest to the area of operations. In addition to the aforementioned attack force, the operation was supported indirectly by a group of air units, including the bombers of the Middle East and the Coastal Air Command, which reached a total of 3,395 aircraft. To conquer the island of Pantelleria, Eisenhower chose the British 1st Infantry Division, which had received training in amphibious warfare in England, but had not been selected for the invasion of Sicily.

On May 9 Palermo was put to fire and sword by a wave of intense and non-stop bombing: during the day a total of 122 B-17 flying fortresses, 89 B-25 Mitchell and B-26 Marauder and, in the night, 23 Vickers Wellington, had altogether unloaded on the Sicilian capital 485 tons of ordnance.

On May 10, the American scouts of the 3rd Photographic Reconnaissance Group USAAF, belonging to the Northwest African Photographic Reconnaissance Wing (NAPRW), headed by Colonel Elliott Roosevelt, son of the more famous President of the United States of America Franklin Delano Roosevelt, while carrying out photographic surveys, had identified 12 aircraft on the airport of Pantelleria, of which 9 fighters were still operational and a large number of aircraft destroyed in previous raids.

The following day, over Sicily, the USAAF 9th Air Force sent 48 B-24 Liberator heavy bombers, 26 of the 98th and 22 of the 376th Bombardment Group, from various airfields in Libya, accompanied by a large escort of 47 RAF Spitfires from Malta. The main target of the bombardment was the port of Catania, where the bombers unloaded in several waves from an altitude between 22,000 and 25,000 feet, depending on the position inside the combat box[2], 230 500 lb. bombs and 60 4 lb. incendiary bombs, for a total of 113 tons of ordnance. The devastating bombardment caused the death of 216 people and the wounding of 303, mostly civilians.

While the final attack on the island of Pantelleria was being planned, the NAPRW, that is the Allied reconnaissance, drew up in June a photographic coverage program even wider than the one used until then and which concerned southern Europe and in particular the city of Rome.

On May 20, the flying fortresses went as far as Grosseto, bombing the airport. On the 21st, the B-24 Liberators of the 9th Air Force attacked Villa San Giovanni and Reggio Calabria. Incursions were carried out over most of southern Italy and Sardinia. The month ended with the bombing of the Foggia airport complex by NASAF B-17s.

On the first of June Pantelleria was attacked by 19 B-17 Flying Fortress heavy bombers of the 97th Bombardment Group USAAF, escorted by 28 P-38 Lightning of the 82nd Fighter Group USAAF. The photographic reconnaissance carried out during the bombardment highlighted the reaction of the coastal defense batteries and pinpointed their exact location. The photos taken were considered excellent by the Intelligence Section personnel, who distributed them as usual to the various air units.

The tactical bombers of the 55 Squadron RAF, the Martin 187 Baltimore, on the basis of this information were called to manage a series of attacks aimed at the defensive positions of the island[3].

On the morning of June 7, the first raid was carried out by a formation of 10 Baltimore of 55 Squadron RAF led by Wing Commander J. F. Roulston from Enfidaville airstrip, joined by 12 Baltimore of the 223 Squadron RAF. The following morning 11 Baltimore of 55 Squadron led by Major J.A. Mouton, escorted by 12 P-40 of the 79th American Fighter Group, went into action and attacked with 500 lb ordnance the gun emplacements along the coast of Pantelleria, a mission that was repeated in the morning and afternoon of June 9. The sorties continued also on the 10th and 11th. On the 12th, the port and the town of Lampedusa saw the attack of a formation of 12 Baltimore of 55, led again by Wing Commander J. F. Roulston DFC, commander of the 232 Wing RAF.

By June 11, the NATAF had flown a total of 728 sorties in 63 missions against Pantelleria, and 154 sorties in 14 missions against Lampedusa. In all, nearly 1,100 aircraft participated in the final assault, dropping 1,571 tons of bombs, for a total, for the period from June 1 to 10, of 4,844 tons of ordnance, distributed in 3,647 sorties. From the 8th of May to the 11th of June, the Northwest African Air Forces (NAAF) carried out a total of 5.285 sorties, at the expense, for the Allied forces, of 16 damaged aircrafts and 14 lost, for a total of 6.200 tons of bombs launched.

---

2 The combat box, also known by the term "staggered formation" was the tactical combat formation used by the heavy strategic bombers of the United States Army Air Force during World War II. The advantages of this formation were many, both from a defensive point of view, with the ability to provide great firepower with the heavy machine guns of the bombers, but also from an offensive point of view with the ability to drop the war load in a short time on the objective.

3 The Martin 187 Baltimore was an American-built twin-engine light bomber. Developed at the request of the Royal Air Force, it was employed during World War II. It went into action in the spring of 1942, alongside other RAF light bombers in the Mediterranean. The adaptation of the pilots to the new machine, however, was neither quick nor easy. Because of the power of the engines, very high compared to the weight, take-off was particularly dangerous. It was precisely in an accident on this aircraft that the Italian torpedo ace, Carlo Emanuele Buscaglia, lost his life and died the following day in the British military hospital in Naples on August 24, 1944. Although the Baltimore was never employed by any U.S. military force, it was still designated A-30.

OPERATION HUSKY

On July 6 Wing Commander L. J. Joel personally led the first attack for the 55 Squadron in the Sicilian Campaign. While all personnel had moved to the Reyville airstrip near the Gulf of Hammamet, Tunisia, two formations of six Baltimore aircraft each, escorted by 24 Warhawks of the 324th Fighter Group USAAF, raided the dispersal areas of Trapani Milo airport, dropping 72 250 lb. bombs on them from an altitude of 10,500 feet. The German-Italian flak defending the airport proved to be particularly intense, precise and heavy. Shortly after opening the holds and releasing the ordnance, the Baltimore FA232 "A" piloted by Lieutenant J. Wilkinson was seen to lose altitude. A few moments later three parachutes were noticed as the aircraft crashed into the surrounding hills. Seven bombers also suffered minor anti-aircraft damage, with one of them heavily damaged.

The 55 Squadron's missions on the same target were repeated on the morning of the following day; this time the formation of 12 Baltimore aircraft led by Major J. A. Mounton suffered no losses, but had to face a fierce attack by some Italian Macchi MC.202s and some German FW190s, on which the 24 Warhawks of the 324th Fighter Group promptly dived.

Already at 03:20 hrs of July 9, a German reconnaissance aircraft had sighted about ninety ships, mostly landing craft, southeast of Pantelleria. A few hours later, at 06:35, another Luftwaffe scout spotted two large units west of Malta, but a blanket of fog prevented it from checking more accurately the waters between the Maltese island and Pantelleria. At 11:00 a.m. a new reconnaissance confirmed the previous suspicions and identified, this time, 12 steamers and 8 patrol boats in front of Cape Bon, and three warships of unspecified type east of Kelibia. Finally, a Bf 109 of the II Fliegerkorps reported five convoys with about 150-200 units, including LCTs and escorts, north of Gozo. At the head of the largest convoy, moving northwest of Malta with about 80 ships, the silhouettes of two heavy units, presumably battleships, were unmistakable. Another 69 ships, including large merchantmen and smaller units, had been photographed in the port of Bizerte some time before. The roadstead of Biserta was checked again a couple of hours later by two Macchi MC.202s from Sardinia, which confirmed the presence of a large number of small ships. Also, the German Junkers Ju 88 scouts, coming from Frosinone and in some cases from Sardinia, had for a long time been meticulously following all Allied naval movements in the Mediterranean, paying particular attention to the coasts north of Algeria; one of them, based in Frosinone but departing from Crotone, crashed for a technical problem to an engine a few miles from Malta at 16:00 of day 7; the crew was taken prisoner[4].

Having evaluated the results of the reconnaissance and the general situation in the central Mediterranean, at 18:00 Supermarina transmitted to the Supreme Command and to the other armed forces the following evaluation of the situation:

"In general fairly favorable weather for simultaneous landing operations in both the southern and eastern coastal areas of Sicily. The considerable number of transport ships and small units in Bizerte and the sighting today in the Malta area of numerous landing craft and heavy forces at sea may indicate the beginning of landing operations during the night.

Two days before, on July 7, German General Adolf Galland had met with Feldmarschall Albert Kesselring and General Wolfram von Richthofen, commander of Luftflotte 2, at the German headquarters in Sicily. The following day Galland affirmed to be by now convinced of the imminent

---

4 Salvo Fagone, *Ricognitori su Husky. Il ruolo cruciale della ricognizione aerea e dell'Intelligence Ultra sulla Sicilia e sul Mediterraneo*, Youcanprint, 2020, p. 187.

Allied landing, and that this at the most would have happened in the turn of the following 48 hours, pointing out moreover not to be in a position to affirm with exactitude where.

On July 9, General Edwin House, head of the XII Air Support Command, called to report all the pilots of the 111th American Tactical Reconnaissance Squadron; the subject was the plan of photographic coverage in the imminence of the Allied landing in Sicily[5]. Also the RAF, for its part, scheduled operations for the Spitfire Tac/Rs of 40 Squadron SAAF, which began their operations on the 9th of July with 3 simultaneous missions over the area south-east of Sicily, in an attempt to determine enemy troop movements along the main road communication routes. It must be underlined that after 8 July no Italian-German movement had been detected near the areas that would have been affected by the landing.

The day before the planned Operation Husky, the Baltimore bombers of the 55 Squadron, together with those of 223 Squadron, returned to the airport of Trapani Milo. At 09:30 the bombers left Tunisia, and a few hours later the 12 Baltimore formation led by Wing Commander L. J. Joel found itself perpendicular to the target. While, at exactly 10:57 a.m., 24 250lb and 500lb bombers rained down from the bombers' holds on the dispersal areas, the heavy anti-aircraft fire, as usual, hit the Baltimore FA331 "L" piloted by Flight Sergeant A. W. Baines which crashed to the ground.

On July 10, 1943, the Axis forces present on the island were under the command of the Italian VI Army, based in Enna, led for about a month by General Alfredo Guzzoni, who had taken over from Mario Roatta, with two Army Corps, XII and XVI. The XII, commanded by General Mario Arisio, based in Corleone, was entrusted with western Sicily, west of the Licata-Cefalù line; the XVI, led by General Carlo Rossi, based in Piazza Armerina, was in charge of the defense of eastern Sicily, from east of Cefalù to Gela. On the eastern side, eyes were focused on the Maritime Military Plaza of Augusta-Siracusa, the impregnable fortress, pride of the Italian Royal Navy, well known to Allied bombers and air reconnaissance. Under the command of General Alfredo Guzzoni more than 200,000 soldiers, of which 32,000 were German, to which were added about 60,000 service men. Many, however, the weak points of these forces, among which the lack of mobility, the inadequate anti-aircraft and anti-tank armament or, still, the regional recruitment of the soldiers, whose morale, especially in the case of the Sicilian ones, could not but suffer from three long years of hunger and war.

In addition to the countless posts used for coastal defense, located between Scoglitti and Licata, and the German Division Hermann Göring in the area of Caltagirone, the Italian-German forces also had the 4th Infantry Division Livorno, placed between Butera and Mazzarino, and the 54th Infantry Division Naples, with the command in Vizzini. Also on 9 July, Spitfires from air reconnaissance of RAF 683 Squadron carried out missions over the cities of Taranto, Naples, Messina and Milazzo.

NASAF, meanwhile, was massively employing a total of 460 bombers, a number that included night bombers, of which 67 Vickers Wellingtons of 205 Group RAF, determined to give the coup de grace to what now remained of the airport installations to the west of the island, and to some important targets, consisting of significant concentrations of Italian-German troops. At 08:17 hrs, twenty-seven B-17 flying fortresses of the 97th Bombardment Group attacked the Sciacca airport. In the same minutes, the airport of Biscari Santo Pietro in Caltagirone was attacked by 26 B-17 Flying Fortresses of the 2nd Bombardment Group and by 25 Flying Fortresses of the 301st Bombardment Group, with 607 500 lb bombs, of which 50% hit the target; the others hit some hangars and other structures east of the airport. Piazza Armerina was hit at 10:55 a.m. by 24 B-26 Marauders of the 319th Bombardment Group, with 144 500 lb bombs. Caltanissetta was the city that suffered the heaviest bombardment: forty-two B-25 Mitchell of the 321st Bombardment Group unloaded, at

---

5 *Ibidem*, p. 188.

17:30, 245 500 lb bombs and 8 300 lb bombs. The intense explosions and the thick cloud of smoke caused by the bombardment impressed the members of the bomber crews so much that they even left a trace in their war diaries. In the city was razed to the ground the Rione Santa Lucia, causing among the civilian population the death of 351 people.

In the early stages of Operation Husky, the Baltimore of the 55th Squadron bombed the airport of Sciacca and carried out armed reconnaissance along some of the roads to the west of the island, focusing mainly on those between Caltanissetta and Agrigento.

At 12:30 p.m. the tactical command of the II Fliegerkorps in Taormina was hit with about 54 tons of explosives launched by 18 B-24 Liberators of the 376th Bombardment Group of the 9th Air Force, killing 45 civilians. At 19:03 it was the turn of the town of Caltagirone, targeted by 27 B-26 Marauder of the 17th Bombardment Group, with 159 bombs of 500 lb. Palazzolo Acreide followed, bombed at 18:28 by 23 B-26 Marauders of the 320th Bombardment Group, with 132 500 lb bombs. During the night it was the turn of the Vickers Wellington bombers and the Handley Page Halifax four-engine aircraft of the Royal Air Force. The first operated several sorties over eastern Sicily and over the airport of Biscari Santo Pietro in Caltagirone. The eight large Halifax four-engine aircraft of the RAAF 462 Squadron, carrying 15 250 lb GP bombs each, took off shortly before midnight from the Hosc Raui air base in Libya, and carried out an attack along the Avola-Noto-San Paolo route, to favour the arrival of the British 1st Airborne Division, for the mission codenamed Operation Ladbroke.

The plan of attack had been elaborated by General Harold Alexander on May 2, during a conference called by General Eisenhower in Algiers. He had established that there would be two landing zones. The area of competence of the American 7th Army, under the command of General George Patton, would have gone from Licata to Scoglitti, for a length of about eighty kilometers. Initially, three Divisions and other minor units would have landed, preceded by the launching of paratroopers of the 82nd American Parachute Division, which would have had to seize some key defense positions. The area of responsibility of the British 8th Army, commanded by General Montgomery (the winner of El Alamein), would have been the one that extends from the Gulf of Noto to Punta Castelluzzo (west of Capo Passero), for over 50 kilometers. In this area would have landed four infantry divisions, two armored brigades and other minor units.

The resistance to the landings of the 8th Army in southeastern Sicily was sporadic and uneven. Perhaps the hardest and most determined resistance was at Avola, where the coastal batteries held the British troops at gunpoint for four hours. The 374th Coastal Battalion was particularly distinguished and its stronghold on the Lido of Avola had to be destroyed with the support of naval artillery.

For the defense of the entire sector of the Augusta-Siracusa stronghold, the commander of the VI Army counted on the rapid intervention of both the Naples Division, gathered in the area of Palazzolo Acreide, and the German Schmalz Motorised Group, which was already moving towards Melilli. Since the situation of the stronghold was apparently much more reassuring than the sector of Gela, Guzzoni preferred to put at disposal of this last one the Divisions Livorno and Herman Göring, however, in the course of the same afternoon the situation in the oriental sector turned quickly to the worse with the fast British advance; the consequence was the sudden abandonment of the stronghold by the Italian troops, an event that left the same Montgomery incredulous.

Patton's troops, initially put in serious difficulty in the area of Gela, quickly re-established the control of the bridgehead, also thanks to the support of an intense naval bombardment against the Italian lines. In a short time, they were able to conquer and work to reactivate the airfields of Comiso, Santo Pietro Caltagirone and Gela Ponte Olivo, and on the British side that of Pachino. Moreover, they prepared to extend the positions in the hinterland, fulfilling the task assigned to protect the left flank of the 8th Army[6]. While in Sicily the Allied ground troops proceeded swiftly, conquering Gela, Syracuse and Augusta, on July 13 the B-24 Liberators of the 9th Air Force bombed the airports of Crotone and Vibo Valentia, with the medium bombers of the NAAF attacking on the island the towns of Leonforte, Randazzo, Termini Imerese and Enna, and the airports of Trapani.

During the night of the 14th, twelve Baltimore of the 55 Squadron were engaged in armed reconnaissance in the area of Agrigento and Misilmeri, with final destination the port of Termini Imerese.

Between the 15th and 16th, two separate missions of six Baltimore each, belonging to the same Squadron, were operated in armed reconnaissance in the roads around Corleone and Villabate, up to Termini Imerese railway station; during the second mission Lercara Friddi, Prizzi, Cianciana and Ribera were also flown over. Several means of transport were identified and attacked along some state routes.

The next night it was the turn of the town of Nicosia and the surrounding areas, on which the 8 Baltimore, led by Warrant Officer R. M. Watkins, dropped 48 250 lb. bombs. On their way back the Baltimore crossed paths with some Junkers Ju 88 bombers returning from a bombing mission against Allied ships off Sicily. A quick exchange of machine gun fire ensued, which according to Squadron sources, led to the shooting down of one of the German bombers as it plunged into flames and exploded on the ground.

The heavy and medium bombers of the 12th Air Force gave no respite to the German and Italian air forces, which had left their last operational bases in the area of Gerbini and Catania, and had positioned themselves in the bases around Foggia, with small formations at Grottaglie, San Pancrazio, Viterbo and Ciampino near Rome. The Luftwaffe's big bombers were decentralized to bases in southern France and northern Italy. The NASAF also hit hard Pomigliano, Montecorvino, Aquino and Capodichino in the Naples area; it did not spare Vibo Valentia, Crotone, Leverano and Grosseto which were located halfway between Rome and Pisa. The effect of these intense attacks was to further reduce the already meager Axis air force in the central Mediterranean, depriving the ground forces of an effective air support in Sicily, both during the maintenance of the defensive line and the subsequent evacuation from the island.

Since July 20, the 55 Squadron had left the airstrip of Reyville, in North Africa, to position itself in the closest one of Luqa, in Malta. From the nearby island of the Knights, in the following days the intervention of the 55 Squadron was particularly solicited with the employment of the Baltimore on the locations of central Sicily, with the bombing of Adrano and Troina on July 22, and Misterbianco and Novara di Sicilia on the 23rd.

After the capture of Palermo, which took place on July 22, the 7th American Army headed east. On the other side of the island, the 1st Canadian Division proceeded with some difficulty in the Enna hinterland. In support of the latter, the Baltimores of the 55 Squadron led by Wing Commander L. J. Joel went into action on July 26, to attack the Italian-German positions near the town of Regalbuto, on which the bombers launched 72 250 lb. bombs. Here, intelligence cooperation and aerial reconnaissance had reported a suspected Italian-German communications center/command. With the American 45th Division advancing along the Tyrrhenian coast less than five miles from Santo Stefano di Camastra, the bombers of the 55 Squadron also acted as a pathfinder between the enemy lines, attacking Milazzo on the morning of July 27 and 29. At the same time, the British 8th Army, was still blocked, since July 20, on the line of the river Dittaino in the plain of Catania, a position conquered in the fierce and bloody fighting near the Primosole bridge, a few kilometers from Catania, and of Sferro and Gerbini.

---

6 Angelo Plumari, *Operazione Husky. La guerra nell'entroterra ennese*, Leonforte (EN), Euno Edizioni, 2019, p. 24.

After having captured some strategic positions, such as Troina in the hinterland of Enna, and Adrano in the area of Catania, the Allies immediately launched a double offensive on the slope of Etna, against Randazzo, the last stronghold of the enemy in the center of the line of the volcano, with the purpose of dividing the Italian-German forces in half, forcing them to the general withdrawal along the two coastal roads in the direction of Messina.

In fact, Patton had already established that if he had to capture Messina, the 7th Army would have needed only two east-west roads passing north of the volcano Etna: road 113, the coastal artery from Palermo to Messina, and road 120, a mountain road passing inland and crossing Sicily from Nicosia to Randazzo[7].

The journey to Randazzo was accompanied by intense air attacks, mostly carried out by the tactical bombing units of the NATAF, under the continuous requests of the ground troops. Randazzo, Paternò, Adrano and Misterbianco quickly became the center of convergence of all air attacks, becoming one of the most heavily bombed targets in Sicily during the second phase of Operation Husky.

On 31 July, while the ground personnel of the 55 Squadron were preparing to reach Sicily and take position on the new airstrip prepared by the engineering units near Monte Lungo, the Baltimore attacked Paternò and Centuripe.

The climax of the bombing of Randazzo was reached on August 7, when 104 B-25 Mitchells and 142 Boston and Baltimore bombers razed the entire city to the ground. The intensity of this war action was never reached or exceeded until the end of the Sicilian campaign. 12 Baltimore aircraft led by Wing Commander L. J. Joel DFC also took part in the operations on Randazzo, bombing the city with 48 500 lb. bombs.

---

7 Carlo D'Este, *1943. Lo sbarco in Sicilia*, Milano, Mondadori, 1990, p. 360.

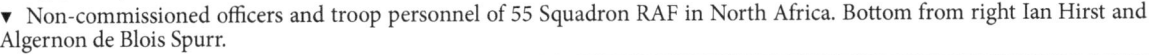

▲ Algernon de Blois Spurr (right) and his brotherly friend Ian Hirst (left), in a souvenir photo that shows them together on two dromedaries in front of the pyramids of Giza. Both belonging to the second photographic unit (2 PRU) of the RAF in Egypt, they will later transit within the 55 Squadron RAF. When Algernon married in 1947, Ian Hirst was his best man.

▼ Non-commissioned officers and troop personnel of 55 Squadron RAF in North Africa. Bottom from right Ian Hirst and Algernon de Blois Spurr.

▲ Officers of 55 Squadron in a customary group photo before leaving Reyville Air Base, Tunisia, to take up position on the runway at Luqa, Malta. The Squadron had closed the North Africa Campaign on May 12, 1943, with its last raid north of Enfidaville. (55 Squadron Association).

▼ The Squadron's Martin 187 Baltimore IIIAs arranged on the airstrip at Fauconnerie, Tunisia, in May. The first Baltimore IIIA 'K' is s/n FA207, generally flown during May operations by Flight Sergeant C. S. Pay.

▲ Algernon de Blois Spurr under the scorching desert heat holding some correspondence.

▲ Self-portrait of Algernon de Blois Spurr.

▲ A car carrying Prime Minister Sir Winston Churchill and General Mark Clark as they review Allied troops shortly after the end of the Tunisia Campaign.

▼ Algernon busy in the maintenance of a field generator set.

▲ Bombing of Pantelleria airfield by a formation of 17 Baltimore of 55 Squadron, led by Squadron Leader E. W Murray DFC, together with 18 Baltimore of 223 Squadron. The formation of 232 Wing RAF, perhaps the most consistent during the Italian Campaign, was escorted by 8 P-40s of the 79th Fighter Group USAAF and 42 Spitfires. British-made F.24 cameras were commonly used for aerial photography.

▼ The harbor and town of Lampedusa, bombed on June 12, 1943 by a formation consisting of 12 Baltimore of the 55 Squadron, personally led by Wing Commander J. F. Roulstone DFC, commander of 232 Wing RAF.

▲ On 6 August 1943, the last aliquots of ground personnel of 55 Squadron, along with those of 232 Wing, prepared for the trip to Sicily.

▼ The ship loaded with the vehicles of 55 Squadron ready to sail.

▲ The arrival in Licata, on 7 August 1943. The town had been conquered by Colonel Truscott's American Joss Force, which had met only weak resistance from the Italian 207th Coastal Division.

▼ Once the vehicles had disembarked, the caravan made its way to the new airstrip set up in the Gela area. The convoy of vehicles left behind Licata driving along SS 123 and the Church of Maria S.S. di Pompei, perched on the hill overlooking the town.

▲ Arrival in Gela. On the building on the right is the inscription indicating the entrance to the city; on the other side of the building is engraved on the wall the phrase of the Fascist period "THE STRONG PEOPLE CAN LOOK AT THE FACE OF THEIR OWN DESTINY".

▼ After experiencing the tragic moments of the landing in Sicily, the children of Gela tried to leave the past behind, returning to play in the streets of the city still deserted.

▲ Other Sicilian girls smiling in front of the camera of the allied soldiers.

▲ After conquering the Axis airport of Gela Ponte Olivo, the American engineers took care of setting up other dirt runways where the airborne units could be stationed, in anticipation of supporting the ground troops in their advance on the Italian mainland. Among them was the runway of Monte Lungo, where the 55 Squadron stopped for a short period of time.

▼ The eighteenth-century mother church of Gela or church of Santa Maria Assunta.

▲ The town of Caltagirone was bombed by 27 B-26 Marauders of the 17th Bombardment Group USAAF with 159 bombs of 500 lb. Here you can see the roofs of some houses in the historic center still uncovered. In the lower right corner you can see a man trying to rebuild the roof of his home.

▼ The city market of Caltagirone, which is still repeated every Saturday of the week.

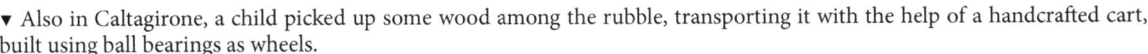

▲ The late baroque church of San Francesco d'Assisi all'Immacolata, or simply church of the Immacolata, together with the ex-convent of the Order of the Friars Minor Conventual, constitutes a monumental pole located in Piazza San Francesco d'Assisi - near the homonymous bridge - in the historical center of Caltagirone. During the bombings, a big bomb missed it, destroying the nearby houses. The explosion however caused huge damages to the structure.

▼ Also in Caltagirone, a child picked up some wood among the rubble, transporting it with the help of a handcrafted cart, built using ball bearings as wheels.

▲ The palace of the Municipality of Catania covered with rubble and without part of the roof. At the center of the square the elephant, symbol of the city.

▼ The Sicilian cart, in Sicilian "carrettu", is a horse-drawn vehicle used for the transport of goods, in use throughout the Sicilian territory from the nineteenth century until the second half of the twentieth century. Built with different qualities of wood, often adorned with bucolic carvings and garish pictorial decorations, nowadays it has become an object of artisan art, as well as one of the symbols of Sicilian folkloric iconography.

▲ A building completely gutted in the center of Catania. The airport of the city was the protagonist of the first air raid on Malta, which took place shortly after the declaration of war by Italy to France and England.

▲ In Lentini, Spurr's camera lens immortalized a uniformed Carabiniere armed with a 91/38 cavalry musket. The Carabinieri were given responsibility for public order in the town after the expulsion of the Fascist mayors.

▲ The Ferdinandea door, after 1860 entitled to Garibaldi, is a triumphal arch built in 1768 in Catania on a project by Stefano Ittar and Francesco Battaglia to commemorate the wedding of King Ferdinand III of Sicily and Maria Carolina of Habsburg-Lorraine. It is located between Piazza Palestro and Piazza Crocifisso, at the end of Via Giuseppe Garibaldi, in the Fortino district, in Catania dialect "Furtinu". It is possible to notice some indications written on the walls of the monument that indicate the direction of the offices of the Allied military departments in the city.

▲ Scenes of daily life in Lentini (SR) in Piazza Umberto I, where the baroque Mother Church of S. Alfio is in the background. Children are seen walking around with little clothing on and no shoes.

▲ Spurr on top of a photo trailer.

▲ Spurr in flight suit holding an F.24 camera. On the rightight: The development of the films took place inside the small photographic trailers that were usually of the type "J" of American manufacture and particularly suitable to be used in the field. Here we see Spurr holding a film being developed.

▼ Bombing of a bridge during Operation Strangle, whose purpose was to disrupt German supply routes into Italy. In order to carry out extremely precise operations on the targets, the operation required the use of medium and light bombers and fighter-bombers.

THE RETREAT FROM SICILY

On the island, the German army under the orders of General Hube successfully implemented the retreat through three defensive lines, taking advantage of the narrowing of the Sicilian territory as it approached Messina. The Germans sabotaged all the vehicles before abandoning them by burning everything they could spare.

On the two sides of the Strait, the Sicilian one and the Calabrian one, the most impressive concentration of anti-aircraft emplacements, the fearsome 88 mm Flak cannons, of the entire conflict was set up. For the defense of the Strait of Messina, Colonel Ernst-Günther Baade put in place as many as five hundred gun ports located on both sides.

From Montgomery's Diary, dated August 7, 1943, the British general expressed more than a few perplexities about the work of his allies in the attempt to counteract the Italian-German escape to the continent: "There has been intense traffic all day on the Strait of Messina, the enemy is undoubtedly beginning to take the stuff away.

I have endeavored to find out what the combined naval-aviation plan intends to do to prevent this retreat; I have not been able to find out. I'm afraid the real issue is that there is no plan. The trouble is that there is no senior control over this campaign.

Cunningham is in Malta; Tedder is in Tunis; Alexander is in Syracuse. It strikes me that anyone would think that a campaign could be conducted in this way, with each of the three commanders of the three arms more than 900 miles apart[8]."

On August 10, the high German officer completed his work, putting in place all the artillery planned and with the preparation of ten well camouflaged and set up landings, able to accommodate the fleet of barges and motor boats, which would lead men and materials in Calabria.

Randazzo fell on August 11, the Italian-German troops had no choice but to quickly cross the Strait of Messina to retreat to the continent.

The 55 Squadron was an eyewitness to the evacuation of the troops from the island; during the final stages of the Sicilian campaign, the Squadron's Baltimores attacked several times the coasts between Sicily and Calabria. On August 12, two formations of six aircraft each bombed a probable Italian-German headquarters near Patti; two days later they aimed at a road junction not far from Palmi; on the 15th twelve Baltimores attacked a concentration of boats near Sant'Agata di Militello. The 16 was carried out by them the last attack of the Campaign of Sicily, with the bombing of two big boats of 7,000 tons each at anchor near Messina, on which were launched 48 bombs of 500 lb.

Captain Gustav Freiherr von Liebenstein, already decorated with the Knight's Cross, was chosen to coordinate the naval operations for the evacuation of the island. At his orders he had three transport flotillas of the Kriegsmarine, similar units of the army, some armed pontoons of the Luftwaffe as well as Italian ships of various sizes[9].

This heterogeneous fleet managed by five battalions of engineers was able to transport 8,000 men and 2,000 tons of materials and equipment every night. A French warship, SG 13, and four 100-ton minesweepers provided the escort while underway.

---

8 Ibidem, p. 444.
9 The main craft was the Siebel pontoon or Siebelfähre, a type of vessel designed in 1940 by the aeronautical engineer Siebel, often armed with 20 mm Flak anti-aircraft guns for self-defense, some were converted to floating anti-aircraft batteries with 88 mm Flak guns. It consisted of two heavy-duty deck elements with propulsion provided by self-propelled engines, with a displacement of 130 tons, a fully loaded speed of 6-7 knots, and a carrying capacity of 50 tons and 150-200 men.

The ferries of von Liebenstein were able to transport:

- 8,615 troops
- 4,489 wounded
- 3,159 vehicles + 3 tanks
- 446 tons of ammunition
- 527 tons of fuel
- 5,155 tons of equipment[10]

According to the German Chief of Staff, Colonel Bogislaw von Bonin: "On the fifth line of defense, the last remaining troops were to go directly to the boats on the last night before the final evacuation. In the area around Messina and in the city itself the divisions were to be assigned clearly defined assembly and embarkation areas. The roads for transfer to those areas and the control of traffic on other roads would also have been indicated with absolute exactitude. Each division was marked the direct route to the ferry and an exact number of boats and ferries. Exact orders had also been given for landing on the mainland and for transfer to the muster areas [...][11]."

At the dawn of 17 August, the evacuation of the island could be said to be concluded with a complete German success. In the course of the 5 days only very few ships and some Siebel pontoons were lost. This was the end of what Allied military historians called the Italian-German Dunkirk and which, it should be remembered, took place for the Italian and German armies simultaneously but in parallel, as the Axis forces each jealously committed their own means to evacuate the island.

On the domestic front, the most intense and spectacular air battle of the month materialized on Monday, August 16, during an attack on the Foggia airport complex by B-24 Liberators of the 9th Air Force. Between 75 and 100 Italian-German fighters engaged in a long fight with the Liberators and the area escort; eight American four-engine aircraft were lost in the battle, claiming the destruction of forty-five enemy fighters. These aerial actions carried out in the final phase of Operation Husky brought the actual sorties to 4,846 and the bombs dropped to 8,009 tons[12].

While in the diary of the 55 Squadron, Wing Commander L. J. Joel wrote that the "coup de grace" had finally been given to the Sicilian Campaign, all the personnel were again preparing to move to the east of the island, towards the new airstrip located on the Catania plain. Joel, in the meantime, pulled the sums of what he himself considered one of the fiercest air battles of the Mediterranean, the Squadron left in fact, between dead and prisoners of war, 15 officers and NCOs. To complicate matters, there were also outbreaks of Malaria that unfortunately debilitated the personnel.

The fall of Sicily was sealed by the entry of the 3rd Infantry Division of the 7th U.S. Army of General Patton, that at 10:00 a.m. of August 17 entered triumphantly in Messina, followed by the British troops of General Montgomery.

---

10 Von Liebenstein's War Diary. British official historians calculated that there were 4,500 vehicles evacuated between August 1 and 10.
11 Carlo D'Este, op. cit., p. 411.
12 For these data the missions operated by all Allied air units against Italian, Sardinian and Sicilian airports between July 4 and August 17 were taken into consideration.

ROME IS BOMBED

The salvation of Rome had for too long been tolerated by the Allies, invoked by Pope Pius XII and exploited by the Duce, who did not follow the only path that could certainly have spared it the shame of bombing: demilitarize it. All the centers of power, of command, all the bodies of the State were instead enclosed in that perimeter lapped by the waters of the Tiber, in the shadow of the Colosseum and the Basilica of St. Peter's in the Vatican.

The bombing of Rome was an old British dream, not achieved yet mainly because of technical difficulties, however, began to take shape when the landing in French North Africa, Operation Torch of November 8, 1942, put in the hands of Allied air bases closer to the target. Just 5 days after the beginning of the operation Torch, a note of the Foreign Office clarified exactly the terms of the question, according to the point of view of the British government: "if we bomb Rome [...] this will be for political and psychological reasons [...], [this fact] would put Italy in more turmoil than the bombing of any other city. The best course of action is then to keep this card to play and to use it at the end of a campaign aimed at provoking a revolution in Italy[13]".

In the summer of 1943, the scruples that had restrained British Prime Minister Churchill and his Foreign Minister Eden from bombing the eternal city had come to an end and the Allies decided to launch a large-scale punitive and demonstrative action[14]. Already Eisenhower, at the time of the invasion of Sicily, had said clearly that it was landing on a land rich in historical and architectural evidence, but had also added that no monument was worth the life of a single soldier.

The incursion was prepared with the utmost care. Repeated photographic reconnaissance provided the material to prepare special maps in which the objectives to be attacked and the areas to be respected were carefully marked. A reconnaissance carried out by the NAPRW on July 12 made it possible to draw on a map the position of 148 anti-aircraft guns within and outside the city perimeter. A rough estimate, in fact, reported that Rome was defended by 45 batteries with about 220 guns. The deployment was also reinforced by three Flak batteries with 88 mm pieces, which were served as usual by commanded firing stations and search and targeting radars.

The bombing of Rome had a preamble, entrusted to the Vickers Wellingtons of 205 Group RAF. It was they, in fact, who around one o'clock in the morning of 19 July attacked the airports of Frosinone, Tarquinia and San Biagio. Two and a half hours later, some of them launched 800,000 leaflets into Rome announcing the imminent bombing of the city. Although the few hours of notice were not enough for such a large population to evacuate the city in a timely manner, the Allies took care to deliver the announcement that could *create a favorable psychological effect*[15].

JULY 19TH 1943

The humidity in the Capitoline city was 38° in the shade, with a significant upward trend. It had not been so hot in Rome for at least five years according to statistics. Large American air forces had been flying in from North Africa for a few hours. At those altitudes, over 20,000 feet, unlike the Roman temperature, the men aboard the bombers were well covered with padded jackets and gloves.

---

13 Public Record Office Fo 371-33228, November 13th 1942, (citato da M. Gioannini e G. Masobrio in "Bombardate l'Italia. Storia della guerra di distruzione aerea 1940-1945", Rizzoli, 2007, Milano, p. 331.
14 Anthony Eden served as British Foreign Secretary for several terms, and then from 1955 to 1957 he became Prime Minister.
15 The History of the Twelfth Air Force, Pantelleria, Sicily, p. 118 (AFHRA A-6202).

The first bombardment of the capital began at 11:03 a.m. and ended at 1:35 p.m. on July 19, and was carried out in two phases: from 11:03 a.m. to 12:10 p.m. on the Littorio and San Lorenzo railway stations as primary targets, from 12:12 p.m. to 1:35 p.m. on the Littorio and Ciampino airports. The formations of the four-engined and twin-engined aircraft of the 12th and 9th Air Force arrived in Rome from two directions: from the northwest, entering from the sea between Civitavecchia and Ladispoli, turning right towards the city, and from Nettuno, penetrating the coast south of the city and continuing straight towards Ciampino. By doing so, the work of the spotters was favored and they found themselves all targets lined up on the same slightly transversal axis: the Littorio area on the Salaria, the Tiburtino-San Lorenzo district, the airport area of Ciampino on the Appia.

Over Rome, in the late morning, four groups of B-17 Flying Fortresses of the 5th Bombardment Wing of NASAF, and groups of B-24 Liberators of the 9th Air Force, in all 156 B-17 Flying Fortresses of the 12th and 117 B-24 Liberators of the 9th Air Force took off from Tunisia, Algeria and Libya[16]. The 273 four-engine aircraft pounded the railway junction on the Salaria and the San Lorenzo station for an hour and twenty minutes; a Squadron of Flying Fortresses of the 99th Bombardment Group also targeted the Tiburtino airport, at Portonaccio. Shortly before noon, 117 B-26 Marauders and 144 B-25 Mitchell medium twin-engine bombers also arrived and attacked Littorio and Ciampino airports. Together, the 12th Air Force bombers constituted a substantial air fleet, the most powerful ever assembled over a single city in Italy. Escorting the bombers were P-38 Lightning twin-tailed fighters, which, in the interval between waves, descended at low altitude to machine-gun mainly large squares, such as the piazzali del Verano, largo Preneste and piazzale Prenestino.

Charles Bremser was 23 years old and was piloting a P-38 Lightning fighter named Little Mary. He dived on Piazzale Prenestino: "I was angry because I hadn't met any Italian fighters, you know how we pilots are when we are young, always brawling and wanting to fight. Well, I wanted to fight, I wanted to shoot down my fourth enemy fighter, in the previous days I had shot down two Germans and one Italian. But I didn't meet any. So I asked the patrol leader if I could go down on a free hunt, and I went down. I saw on the big square, and I didn't know until later that it was Prenestino, a lot of people running one way, I don't know where. I ducked down and unloaded long bursts, I saw a few fall, including a couple in green uniforms, soldiers I think.[17]" In a little more than two hours of apocalypse, 1,060 tons of explosives were dropped on Rome, something like 4,000 bombs and incendiary fragments: it was the largest incursion ever carried out on Italy, also in terms of launched tonnage[18].

Carl Spaatz, head of the NAAF, affirmed that "the mission of July 19th over Rome had been a monument to the precision of the American method of bombing[19]". He added that "it had been very uninteresting from the point of view of the air force, because it had been too easy[20]." The first official balance sheet of July 22 will fix the dead at 717 and the wounded at 1,599, but the number of dead and wounded will double[21]. The Duce was hundreds of km away, in Villa Gaggia, near Feltre[22].

16 Andrew Brookes, *Air War over Italy*, Ian Allan, 2000, Shepperton (UK), p. 17.
17 Cesare De Simone, *Venti angeli sopra Roma. I bombardamenti aerei sulla città eterna. 19 luglio e 13 agosto 1943*, Milano, Mursia, 1993, p. 172.
18 The tragic record will pass less than a month later in Milan, where on the night of August 13, RAF Lancasters and Halifaxes will drop 1,904 tons of bombs and another 1,534 tons two nights later.
19 The History of the Twelfth Air Force, Pantelleria, Sicily, p. 120 (AFHRA A-6202).
20 Craven Wesley Frank, *The Army Air Force in World War II*, The University of Chicago Press, 1949, p. 463.
21 Bulletin n. 1,151 of July 20 reads: The damages caused by the American formations, that with some hundreds of four-engine aircraft attacked Rome yesterday, during three hours, are huge; among the others, buildings sacred to worship and science and neighborhoods of workers' houses are seriously hit and partly destroyed: in particular the Basilica of San Lorenzo, the Verano cemetery, the University City, the hospital complex of the Policlinico, the public housing in the Prenestina and Latina areas. The number of civilian victims ascertained so far is 166 dead and 1659 wounded. During and after the raid the population gave an example of discipline and calm.
22 Hitler and Mussolini, in the ten years from June 14, 1934 to July 19, 1944 met seventeen times. The meeting of 19 July 1943 will pass into history as "The meeting of Feltre", although Villa Socchieva (from the Latin "sub clivo" from its posi-

Arthur Hooper was a reporter for the Reuter Agency and was one of the six journalists, two British and four American, who had been allowed to participate in the raid on Rome aboard the Flying Fortresses. Hooper was on board the B-17 Black Bison. His report was published in almost every newspaper in the States. Among other things, he wrote: "The first flying fortresses that have flown over the Italian capital have successfully hit their targets. I am above Rome as a passenger on board a fortress. Far below me a large column of smoke rises in the cloudless sky to a height of four thousand meters. To get us to the target, we passed over the peaceful Italian coast and the Lido, on which numerous fishing boats were floating. The villages, the valleys, the rivers, all the Roman countryside suffer at our sight. From a distance the lake of Monterosi looks like a mirror in the sun. I look at the clock, it's 11:30. We follow the first waves of fortresses. We are over four thousand meters above sea level and the massive dome of St. Peter's Basilica is already clearly outlined in the distance.

A few moments before arriving at the target, the door is opened. Suddenly numerous bombs fall, followed by those of the other aircraft. On the ground we can see clouds of smoke and fire. One of our planes is damaged, but it can still fly. In uninterrupted waves the four-engine aircraft burst in unison on their targets[23]". The basilica of San Lorenzo fuori le Mura, which enjoyed extraterritoriality, had been reduced to ruins and would become a symbol of the Roman tragedy when Pope Pius XII, exceptionally leaving the Vatican by car, spread his arms, then joined his hands in prayer, knelt down and intoned the De profundis. His Rome, the Holy City of Catholicism, had not been spared despite his intercession.

On the morning of July 21, L'Osservatore Romano wrote: "His Holiness, as soon as he was informed of the serious damage to the district of San Lorenzo and to the Tiburtino, Prenestino and Latino quarters, and to the Patriarchal Basilica of San Lorenzo, went there... in a very private way, without any escort, without even forewarning the dignitaries of the Court, only with Monsignor Giovanni Battista Montini, substitute of the Secretariat of State[24]". Vittorio Emanuele III and Queen Elena were also present, as well as a million liras to be distributed to the poor families of the capital, affected by the air raids. The soldier king had been brooding for some time on how to get rid of Mussolini, fascism and all the consequences that, for the first time, he saw with his eyes accustomed to not letting his emotions show.

At 02:30 in the morning of July 25, after ten hours of discussion, the majority of the hierarchs of the Great Council of Fascism voted no confidence in the Duce, Benito Mussolini. At 17:30 of the same day Mussolini was arrested by the Carabinieri, thus decreeing the end of the fascist regime. The Badoglio government had already asked the United States, through the Vatican, to know the essential conditions to obtain for Rome the status of open city; Eisenhower had to wait for further instructions before authorizing a second bombing. Of course, the hypothesis of granting Rome the status of open city had aroused the violent opposition of Churchill, who had pointed out to Roosevelt its political inappropriateness since it would have been taken as proof that the Allies were abandoning the principle of unconditional surrender[25].

---

tion under the hill) or Pagani-Gaggia, summer residence of the senator of the kingdom Achille Gaggia (who with Volpi and Cini will be interpreter of the industrial take-off after the war of Sade, then became Enel), is actually in San Fermo, an isolated town outside Belluno, about twenty kilometers from Feltre. The error, then approved by the official historiography, is probably due to a banal misprint of Mussolini himself, who in his memoirs remembers it as "meeting of Feltre". Hitler took the floor in the main hall of the villa, in front of an apathetic Mussolini, present the undersecretary Bastianini, the ambassadors Von Mackenzen and Alfieri, the chief of staff General Ambrosio, Field Marshal Keitel, General Rintelen, General Warlimont, Colonel Montezemolo, Schmidt and others of the entourage. A cold monologue, with a long inventory of things that Italy had not done, or had done badly. After half an hour the Duce intervened to translate into German the message of the bombing of Rome.

23 In: Rust Kenn C., *Twelfh Air Force story in World War II*, Londra, Hersant, 1967.
24 Giovanni Battista Montini will be the future Pope Paul VI.
25 Roosevelt Churchill, *Carteggio segreto di guerra*, A. Mondadori Editore, Milano 1977, p. 407.

AUGUST 13TH, 1943

Twenty-four days after the first bombing, Rome was hit for the second time. At 11:00 a.m. on Friday, August 13, American planes arrived in geometric formations enclosed within the combat box. They all belonged to the USAAF 12th Air Force, which took off from the airports of Tunisia and Algeria[26], and were accompanied by fighter escorts coming from the airport of Pantelleria and from the Sicilian bases. There were 106 B-17 flying fortresses escorted by 45 P-38 Lightnings, to which were added 102 B-26 Marauders and 66 B-25 Mitchell escorted by 90 P-38 Lightning fighters. A total of 409 planes flew over the capital at various altitudes and in less than an hour unloaded 500 tons of explosives, which was half the amount of bombs that had been dropped during the entire day of July 19.

The B-17 Dirty Gertie of the 32nd Bombardment Squadron, 301st Bombardment Group USAAF, had been boarded by General Doolittle, who this time had ended up leading the raid personally. It was his second raid on Italy for the man who had bombed Tokyo, as the newspapers now called him?; the previous May 18th, aboard a Vickers Wellington, he had participated in a raid on Alghero, Sardinia. The bombing lasted an hour and a half, with a cease-fire at 12:33.

The Romans had been displaced in the towns of Lazio: tens of thousands of people who, when night fell, went to sleep in the shelters, leaving the houses empty and the same scenes of fear that in those war years had been repeated in the cities of southern Italy, such as Naples, Palermo and Catania just to name a few, now afflicted the population of the eternal city.

The second bombing of Rome was inserted, militarily speaking, in the context of the offensive unleashed by the U.S. Air Force in the Mediterranean from the beginning of August to prepare the ground for the path towards its conquest. The plan included large-scale bombings against ports, stations, airports, railway lines and communication routes. From a political point of view, it was clear that by now Eisenhower, in agreement with his government and the British, was trying to accelerate Badoglio's decision to sign an armistice and bring Italy out of the conflict.

The primary objectives of the flying fortresses were to give a "clean sweep" to the Littorio and Ciampino airports, the San Lorenzo freight yard and the Tuscolana station, and to wipe out the Prenestina and Casilina stations. This time the Tuscolano and Casilino districts were in the grip of the bombers, although Portonaccio and San Lorenzo were not spared. Between piazza Ragusa and piazza Lodi, on the axis of via Enna, not even the streets and the squares were spared: about thirty buildings completely collapsed, five of them on fire, almost all the others riddled with splinters and damaged by the air displacement. Very serious damages in via Melfi, via Oristano, via Avezzano, via Montepulciano, via Taranto, via della stazione Tuscolana. In via Melfi 80 people were trapped in a shelter; the rescue teams managed to get only 24 out; in via Montepulciano, on the sidewalk of building number 15, the bodies of all those who lived there were lined up: four families, 19 people.

At the Casilino bridge on the railway line coming from Naples, two bombs hit the tracks and blocked them, overturning the engine, a long convoy bound for Terni with 1,200 soldiers repatriated from Italian East Africa on board.

In via Mirandola, a bomb hit the church of Santa Maria dell'Orto, with an institute of nuns attached: about twenty worshippers and some nuns, who were praying in the church, managed to escape a few seconds before the explosion. Also, at the Casilino a Spanish nunnery with annexed

---

[26] The B-24 Liberators of the 9th Air Force did not take part in this last mission because they were rather debilitated after the heavy losses suffered during the famous and costly raid of 1 August on the Ploiești oil installations in Romania.

boarding school was hit; some of the arches of the Claudio aqueduct were shattered at the level of Via Lanusei. Several arches were blown away by the nearby detonation of a 250-pound bomb, leaving a chasm opened by the explosion. The Aurelian Walls outside the walls of San Giovanni were also hit in two sections. A little further up, a bomb fell on the square in front of the church of Santa Croce in Gerusalemme, collapsing the entire window of the white baroque facade, and knocking down the building at number 11.

The Torpignattara area was machine-gunned and broken up. Here a bomb hit a warehouse of tricolour flags, scattering the drapes and poles around, as if to recall the fall of a nation.

A flurry of bombs and incendiary fragments took Via La Spezia by storm, reducing it to a tangle of collapsed houses. The nearby streets were also devastated by the explosions. In via Orvieto, a bomb penetrated through the window of a top floor and devastated the building up to the foundations; in via Foligno, besides the buildings razed to the ground, the facades of all the houses showed the signs of the machine-gun fire and of the shrapnel, while fires broke out in many buildings in piazza Camerino, via Savona, via Lanusei and via Nola.

In via Caltagirone three bombs one after the other hit the barracks of the Guardia di Pubblica Sicurezza named after Carlo Smiraglia, at number 6, completely without shelter or basements. All the agents who were in the building at the time had taken refuge in the security cells, which seemed to have more solid walls. The bombs caused the collapse of the internal buildings, knocking down the sheds where the vehicles were piled up, sweeping away the surrounding wall and causing the entire escarpment behind the internal building to collapse. The building at number 94 on Via Prenestina was hit by a bomb that took away a slice of it, almost as if a large blade had cut a slice of the building. The Pigneto area, between Casilina and Prenestina, was hit again. The bombs hit the houses that had already suffered the scourge of July 19: Via Macerata, Via Grosseto, Via Avellino, Via Perugia, Via Ascoli Piceno and Via Campobasso. On Via Flaminia two Lightnings dived down to a height of 10 meters to machine-gun a group of people who were running towards the shelter. In the Tor di Quinto area several houses were broken up. In the Porta Mayre area several bombs hit the railwaymen's houses between Via Grattoni, Via Sommeliers and Via Grandis. The façade of the Church of Saints Sebastiano and Veneziano was hit by the air movement and was damaged. The buildings of the Pharmacological Institute and Villa Serventi were hit. For the second time, 250 pound bombs fell on the areas of Portonaccio, San Lorenzo and Prenestino devastated by the first bombardment.

On the morning of August 14, less than 24 hours after the bombing, the Badoglio government declared Rome an open city. It was Foreign Minister Raffaele Guariglia to communicate this to the governments of London and Washington, and to the neutral countries.

ITALY SURRENDERS

The conquest of Sicily in thirty-eight days was in many ways an exemplary campaign. In it, land, air and sea forces had been combined. The main strategic targets of the NASAF bombers, after the Sicilian targets, had been Villa San Giovanni, Salerno, Paola, Marina di Catanzaro, Battipaglia, Sapri and Naples on the Tyrrhenian coast, reaching Rome and Bologna.

Operations for the 55 Squadron, which had ended on August 16 with the bombing of targets around Messina, resumed early in the afternoon of the 26th with an attack by a formation of six Baltimore aircraft at Villa San Giovanni, under the leadership of Wing Commander L. J. Joel DFC. In the meantime, the Squadron moved, through the Sicilian hinterland, to the new Gerbini airstrip

No. 3, better known today as the NATO base of Sigonella. On the 28th, twelve Baltimores of the 55 Squadron attacked Lamezia, while on the 30th and 31st they bombed Catanzaro, thus closing the month just ended.

The landing strip of Sigonella was located in the center of the plain of Catania and took its name from the homonymous district. Sprinkled with craters of previous Allied bombings and wreckage of aircraft destroyed or abandoned, it was actually an old runway used by the men of the Royal Air Force during the war years just passed. On the third of the many satellites of the mother airport of Gerbini, as they were called by the Allied Intelligence, the tragedy of the Italian units of the Regia Aeronautica of the 4th Fighter Wing "Cavallino Rampante" took place on July 5th 1943, with the loss in battle of two Italian Aces, Captain Franco Lucchini and Second Lieutenant Leonardo Ferrulli.

The month of September began with the attempt to weaken the Italian-German rearguards in Calabria, with the bombardment by the 55 Squadron of some military and artillery positions near the small town of Sinopoli, in the province of Reggio Calabria. At 10:48 a.m. of the following day 12 Baltimore of the Squadron, together with 12 Baltimores of 223 Squadron, bombed German positions near Sambatello; in the afternoon it was the turn of a probable Italian-German headquarters near Feroleto della Chiesa, a mission in which 12 Baltimores of 223 Squadron RAF took part, sharing the same air base in Sicily.

Also on September 2, 24 B-17 Flying Fortresses hit far away Bolzano, destroying a bridge and a section of railway line, while another 19 B-17s did the same to two bridges and the railway line near Trento. As a result, communications with the Brenner pass were temporarily blocked; if the operation had been more energetic, continuous and, above all, carried out in due time, it might have delayed the arrival in Italy of the powerful German occupation force, which first the weak Italian government and then the Allied commanders had to deal with. In the afternoon of the same day, 76 B-17 flying fortresses attacked Bologna, unloading 187 tons of bombs, reducing the large railway station to ashes and damaging the historical center of the city.

At 04:30 a.m. of September 3, 1943 (a day marked by the signing of the Italian armistice) a heavy bombardment began on the coast between Reggio Calabria and Villa San Giovanni; at 05:40 a.m. two divisions landed on the Calabrian coast: the British 8th Army and the Canadian 1st Division, thus beginning Operation Baytown. The German resistance was almost nil because the troops had retreated inland between the peaks of the Calabrian Apennines, as they had decided to organize the defenses further north. At 7:30 a.m. the other boats departed from Santa Teresa di Riva and the embarkation was concluded.

The operation had been decided since August 14, 1943, when it was found that the port of Messina was unserviceable because of German sabotage and that for the bulk of the forces, it would be difficult to reach the city of the Strait because of the fact that in the highway between Catania and Messina the Germans in retreat had blown up some bridges with dynamite.

L'Avvenire d'Italia wrote about Operation Baytown: "The enemy is renewing the tactical plan experimented with in Sicily: systematic air attacks on all the railway lines, the military system and the productive centers, through raids that in recent weeks have covered, day and night, without respite, our charming southern provinces".

On September 3, Marshal Badoglio, for the first time officially informed the Chiefs of Staff of the Army, Navy and Air Force that his government was negotiating an armistice with the Allies, which would become effective no earlier than September 12[27]. However, negotiations with the Allies should not have been a mystery to the Italian generals, since on the morning of September 2 Castellano had returned from Sicily aboard an airplane piloted by Major Giovanni Vassallo of the

---

[27] Ruggero Zangrandi, *1943: l'8 settembre*, Feltrinelli editore, Milano, 1967, p. 82.

Aeronautical Staff, who had also been part of the Italian delegation, not to mention the previous contacts with the Allies and other flights to Sicily recorded since the end of August.

In the afternoon of September 3, in a military tent among the olive trees of Cassibile, in the Syracuse area, the flashes of the photographic lenses and the cold eye of the camera immortalized in a brief ceremony, with the cordiality that the circumstances demanded, the signing of an armistice that put an end to the war between Italy and the Anglo-Americans.

The signatures, affixed at 5:15 p.m., were those of Brigadier General, attached to the Italian Supreme Command, Giuseppe Castellano, representing Italian Marshal Pietro Badoglio, Head of Government, and U.S. Army General and Chief of Staff, Walter Bedell-Smith, representing Commander in Chief of Allied forces Dwight Eisenhower.

Castellano signed in full force and effect the so-called short armistice, articulated in twelve points:

"1) Immediate cessation of all hostile activity by the Italian Armed Forces.

2) Italy will make every effort to refuse to the Germans everything that could be used against the United Nations.

3) All prisoners and internees of the United Nations will be handed over immediately to the Allied Commander-in-Chief, and none of them may now, or at any time, be transferred to Germany.

4) Immediate transfer of the Italian fleet and aircraft to such places as shall be designated by the Allied commander-in-chief, with such details of disarmament as shall be fixed by him.

5) Italian merchant shipping may be requisitioned by the Allied commander in chief to meet the needs of his naval military program.

6) Immediate surrender of Corsica and all Italian territory, both islands and mainland, to the Allies, to be used as bases of operation and for other purposes, according to the decisions of the Allies.

7) Immediate guarantee of the free use by the Allies of all airports and naval ports in Italian territory, regardless of the development of the evacuation of Italian territory by German forces. These naval ports and airports will have to be protected by the Italian Armed Forces until this task is assumed by the Allies.

8) Immediate recall to Italy of the Italian Armed Forces from all participation in the war, in any area in which they are currently engaged.

9) Guarantee by the Italian government that, if necessary, it will employ all its available forces to ensure the prompt and precise execution of all conditions of the armistice.

10) The commander in chief of the Allied Forces reserves the right to take whatever measures he deems necessary for the protection of the interests of the Allied Forces, for the prosecution of the war, and the Italian government undertakes to take such administrative and other measures as may be requested by the commander in chief and in particular the commander in chief will establish an Allied military government over those parts of Italian territory where he deems it necessary in the military interests of the Allied nations.

11) The commander in chief of the Allied Forces will have full right to impose measures of disarmament, demobilization and demilitarization.

12) Other conditions of a political, economic and financial nature, which Italy will have to undertake to carry out, will be transmitted later.

The conditions of this armistice will not be made public without the approval of the allied commander in chief[28]".

---
28 Marco Patricelli, *op. cit.*, p. 272.

A first draft of the conditions to be imposed on Italy had been sent from London to Washington on July 29, and the 17 articles had been reduced under pressure from the Americans. The Allies had then elaborated in Quebec, between the 14th and the 24th of August, the explanatory and interpretative text in 44 articles, that will become the so-called long armistice.

The armistice was then made public at 7:45 p.m. on September 8 by the EIAR[29] microphones, which interrupted their broadcasts to transmit the announcement, previously recorded, of General Badoglio's voice announcing the surrender to the nation.

▲ A family of evacuees crammed into a wagon. Note the absence of adult men, except for the elderly gentleman. All the adult and not-so-old men had in fact been called up for war.

---

29 The Italian Radio Audition Board.

▲ Towards the end of August 1943, the 55 Squadron left the Monte Lungo airstrip at Gela to relocate to the Gerbini satellite n. 3, also called Sigonella. Near the new base of the Squadron there were other old Axis airstrips, including satellite No. 9, for the Italian-German Spinasanta. Here, the shot portrayed "The Western Brothers", a British comic-musical duo posing on the wreckage of a German Messerschmitt Bf 109 G-4 "Schwarze 12" fighter belonging to I./JG 53 W.Nr. 19195.

▼ The two comedians filmed while they mocked the now defunct fascist regime by performing an ironic Roman salute astride the German fighter jet.

▲ On September 6, 1943, to cheer the Allied troops deployed in the plain of Catania, was organized a musical show in which there were also the musical duo Beryl Ingham and George Formby.

▲ The two English artists in front of the amused Allied troop.

▼ From his tent at Sigonella, the young Spurr filmed the sudden eruptive activity of the volcano Etna.

▲ The immense panorama of the Etna volcano, the result of a photographic collage of yesteryear. In addition to the countless tents and vehicles, the Baltimore 232 Wing scattered throughout the camp.

▼ The city of Messina. On the wall of a public building reads: "THE PARTY IS THE ARTIFICIAL OF THE REVOLUTION, THE DORSAL SPIN OF THE REGIME, THE MOTOR OF NATIONAL ACTIVITIES".

▲ The 55 Squadron moved towards the Italian peninsula along the Sicilian coast road towards Messina. Here it portrayed the Castle of Sant'Alessio Siculo.

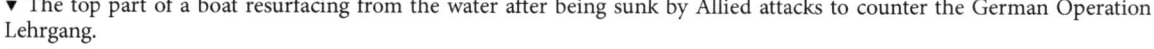

▲ To Spurr's eyes, the city of Messina appeared like a spectre. It had been devastated by bombing since the beginning of the conflict because of its nerve center position.

▼ The top part of a boat resurfacing from the water after being sunk by Allied attacks to counter the German Operation Lehrgang.

▲ Spurr crosses the Strait of Messina with the other members of the Squadron.

▲ Mosaic of Rome, obtained by putting together the photos taken by the aerial reconnaissance by the NAPRW. The targets to be hit and those to be avoided were marked and highlighted. (NARA)

▲ The bombs dropped by an American bomber are about to hit the Testaccio district in Rome. On the right you can see the Porta San Paolo train station in Rome. (NARA)

▼ San Lorenzo station shrouded in explosions. (NARA)

▲ The B-26 Marauder s/n 41-3157 "Little Chun," individual code 28, filmed dropping its Roma ordnance. Belonging to the 442nd Bombardment Squadron, 320th Bombardment Group, this aircraft was severely damaged by anti-aircraft fire during the 20 March 1945 mission to Alberschweiler. The pilot, Lieutenant Edwin B. Gustafson, was able to land the plane at Dijon with the crew unharmed, but the plane was destroyed. (NARA)

▼ Lt. Charles R. Wardwell completed 50 missions with the "Dirty Gertie" s/n 42-5143. Assigned to the 301st Bombardment Group, it was later transferred to the 99th Bombardment Group USAAF. The bomber participated in the bombing of Rome. (NARA)

▲ By the end of September most of the Squadron's personnel had left Gerbini No. 3 to deploy to the new airstrip near Brindisi. On September 28, thanks to the support of DC3s provided by RAF 117 Squadron, the transfer to the new runway was completed. The journey of the aircraft was not easy. During the retreat from Calabria, as had also happened in Sicily, the Axis troops had destroyed almost all road and railroad bridges, making the advance of Allied vehicles difficult.

▼ The photographic trailer crosses a small river in Calabria.

▲ The arrival in Scilla, with a view of the Ruffo castle of Scilla, sometimes also known as the Ruffo castle of Calabria. On the beach a long line of barbed wire and a lone fishing boat surrounded by people.

▼ In the small port of Scylla one can also see an almost destroyed boat and what appears to be a pontoon damaged by probable Allied air attacks in the final phase of Operation Husky.

THE WAR CONTINUES

After the signing of the armistice, General Mark Wayne Clark, who was in command of the American 5th Army, was informed by Eisenhower of the surrender of Italy, and the end of the Italian-German alliance.

The American command planned to launch near Rome the 82nd Parachute Division, codenamed Operation Giant II. This operation, however, was strongly conditioned by the cooperation of the Italian forces, which would have had the task of occupying the airports of Guidonia, Littoria, Cerveteri and Furbara, and make them available to the paratroopers. Unfortunately, Badoglio, who at first seemed to be available for the operation, had some second thoughts and a message followed saying: "Due to the changes in the situation, which has worsened considerably, and due to the presence of German forces in the area of Rome, it is no longer possible to announce the armistice because the capital would be occupied and the Germans would take power by force. The operation is no longer possible because I do not have the necessary forces to maintain the airports".

Meanwhile, the preparations for the conquest of Salerno, codenamed Operation Avalanche, discussed and finalized on August 23 in Algiers, were now in their final stages. The British 8th Army would act as a diversion while the main effort would be made by the American 5th Army at Salerno. The landing force would be composed of General Ernest Dawley's US VI Corps. These forces would have had to conquer Naples and join up with the British 8th Army of Montgomery, coming up from Calabria.

In all the Allied forces could count on about 30,000 British soldiers and 25,000 Americans to attack the German positions, defended by about 20,000 men, already deployed in the area of Salerno, while other 100,000 were the enemies that the Allies believed could converge in the area of the landings in a short time.

These forces put together by the Allies would have had to contrast the 16th Panzer-Division, guided by the German General Heinrich von Vietinghoff that had four divisions, all at a short distance from the bridgehead: after the experience in Sicily in fact, von Vietinghoff decided not to fight on the beaches, but to strengthen his forces and attack, taking advantage of the highest positions. Thus, it was decided that the XIV Panzerkorps would be deployed to the north against the British forces of the X Corps, while the LXXVI Panzerkorps would engage the Americans south of the Sele. The Hermann Göring Armored Division, back from the Sicilian Campaign and reinforced by elements of the 1st Fallschirmjäger Division, with the 15th Panzergrenadier Division, deployed north on the Gulf of Gaeta, but severely short of armor, received the order to move towards the bridgehead already on the evening of September 9.

In support of the American troops landed in Salerno, the 55 Squadron carried out targeted missions on some road links near Auletta, where the anti-aircraft proved to be so accurate and heavy that it hit in 14 different points one of the Baltimores of the formation commanded by Wing Commander L. J. Joel, who was able to return to Sicily. Concentrations of enemy troops were attacked by the Squadron at Eboli on September 14, and at Contursi on September 16, with 12 Baltimore bombers. The month of activity ended on the morning of September 25, with the Squadron protagonist of the bombing of Serino, on which the formation of twelve Baltimore led by Squadron Leader D. H. Hannah unloaded 33 250 lb. bombs and 22 500 lb. bombs. The Squadron, meanwhile, moved to the Italian peninsula with destination Brindisi, ferrying the Strait of Messina.

After ten days of bitter fighting, the Allies, who had suffered much higher losses than the Germans, were able to get out of the quagmire and reorganize in view of the advance toward Naples, which was conquered only on October 1, 1943. The Germans, at the same time, preferred to retreat in an orderly way towards the north in direction of the fortified line, denominated Volturno line, castled in the impervious Apennine territory to north of the Campania capital, where they prepared themselves to face the Allies in advance.

From Brindisi, the 55 Squadron resumed operations only on October 6, with the bombing of Guglionesi, in the province of Campobasso. On October 11, a formation of 12 Baltimore led by Wing Commander L. J. Joel was already in the air to attack Cassino, but was forced to abandon the mission due to a sudden worsening of weather conditions. In the meantime, Hermann Göring and the 18th Panzer Division were entrenched in the area between Isernia and Mignano; here the hard advance of the US 5th Army required the support of the Baltimores of the 55 Squadron, called to bombard the German positions with a particular load of bombs with a 12-hour delay. The raids continued on Teano, Isernia, Boiano, Mignano Monte Lungo, Formia, Gaeta and Cantalupo. On the 29th, the Squadron moved to the Foggia airstrip; from there twelve Baltimores led by Squadron Leader H. R. Harrison attacked Castel Perroso on the morning of October 30. Here the anti-aircraft fire proved to be particularly heavy, damaging all the aircraft of the formation and causing the death of an entire crew, led by Warrant Officer T. Vair pilot of the Baltimore FA657 'V'.

Having settled almost permanently in Foggia, the Squadron, in the final months of the year, was called into action several times, attacking troop concentrations throughout central Italy, "beating" places like Lanciano on November 28, and Miglianico on December 16.

In the ascent of Italy, the Allied troops, at the end of 1943, were bogged down on the preliminary German defense fronts of the Gustav Line, which cut the peninsula in its narrowest point, between the Garigliano and Sangro rivers, from Gaeta to Ortona passing through the Liri valley and Cassino.

To the west operated the 5th Army of Clark, to the east the 8th Army of Montgomery, both had to reckon with the terrible Apennine winter of which they had no knowledge, and with Kesselring on the opposite front who moved the German units continuously. On December 2, the Luftwaffe, just as it had done on November 1 in the attack on Naples, where it had left behind 144 dead, attacked undisturbed on the port of Bari. On the evening of December 2, 1943, 105 Junkers Ju 88 bombers belonging to the German Luftflotte 2 bombed the Allied transport ships anchored at anchor in the port; the attack caused great losses for the Allies, who had not suffered a surprise air raid of such effectiveness and intensity on one of their ports since the Japanese attack of Pearl Harbor.

TARGET: ROME

At the beginning of 1944 an important change in the Allied leadership of the entire Mediterranean theater took place. The well-tested team was ordered to return to England; General Dwight Eisenhower assumed the position of Supreme Allied Commander for the impending invasion of Normandy, and Air Marshal Sir Arthur Tedder was appointed his deputy. General Sir Bernard Montgomery was to command the Army during the initial stages of the Normandy landings, as was Air Vice Marshal Sir Arthur Coningham, who assumed command of the 2nd Tactical Air Force. The place of the new supreme commander in the Mediterranean was assigned to General Sir Henry Maitland-Wilson, while the command of the Allied air forces in the Mediterranean passed to the American General Ira Clarence Eaker, coming from the 8th Air Force USAAF in England. The 8th Army was taken over by General Sir Oliver Leese and, at the same time, the command of the Allied Tactical Air Force in the Mediterranean was assigned to the American General John Kenneth Cannon. The reorganization of the USAAF elements in the Mediterranean was now practically complete. By 1 January 1944, the 12th Air Force had become a purely tactical arm and secondary to the 15th Air Force.

When General Eaker arrived in the Mediterranean on 14 January 1944, the planned landing at Anzio, codenamed Operation Shingle, was only a week away.

On January 22, 1944, the landing was successfully carried out by the U.S. VI Corps, led by General John Lucas, but overall Shingle did not achieve its initial objectives. The German forces, under the command of Feldmarschall Albert Kesselring, despite the initial surprise, were able to block the advance of the VI Corps and to launch a series of counterattacks, which put in serious difficulty the Anglo-Americans and cost them heavy losses. The long and wearisome position battle that followed in the area of the bridgehead continued until the following spring, when the Germans were forced to retreat after the collapse of the Cassino front. Also in this case, however, the main objective, that is the destruction of the German forces in Italy, was not achieved and the retreating Germans were able to escape from the enemy's grip and rearrange themselves on the Gothic Line, a bulwark that engaged the Allies on the Apennines for months.

At the beginning of January 1944 the 55 Squadron had left the airstrip of Celone, near Foggia, to return to Kabrit, in Egypt. Activities over Italy resumed only at the end of March, when the Squadron, reorganized, positioned itself on the Biferno airstrip, from where it conducted missions over the Terni and Spoleto areas in support of Operation Strangle.

With the arrival of spring, the air operations of the Mediterranean Allied Air Forces (MAAF) increased in intensity. On the 19th of March, the official start of Operation Strangle was given, with the aim of hindering and suffocating all movements and supplies destined to the German troops that were feeding the Gustav Line. All rail and road bridges of tactical interest were systematically hit one after the other.

On March 31, the 55 Squadron participated in its first mission employing a formation of 12 Baltimores led by Wing Commander L. Leon that attacked with 250 and 500 lb. ordnance a bridge just south of Roseto degli Abruzzi. On the same coastline, in the early afternoon another formation of 12 Baltimores of the 55 Squadron, led this time by Squadron Leader F. Brieley, bombed a bridge near San Benedetto del Tronto.

The medium bombers flew 176 missions against railroad targets, 113 of which were against targets on the Florence-Rome line. This was certainly the most important line in central Italy, and it was attacked at twenty-two different points between Florence and Orto, and in nineteen of these bombed targets there were bridges.

The following month began with the attack on April 2 of several road and railroad bridges near Sulmona, an operation conducted by 12 Baltimores in the early morning hours. In the afternoon of the same day, it was the turn of targets south of Terni. In the following days, between April 6 and 7, a series of raids were conducted against the hydro-electric plant near Papigno, east of Terni. Between one mission and another the Squadron took a few days off organizing a soccer match in the town of San Martino and making friends with the civilian population. Several missions were ordered on specific locations reported by aerial reconnaissance, which mostly concerned ammunition depots, machine gun emplacements or camps of German troops. On April 29, a probable ammunition depot near San Valentino Citerione was attacked twice.

On the night of May 2 to 3, Baltimore aircraft of the 55 Squadron operated an air raid along the Adriatic coast between Pescara and Ancona. Allied airborne units were trying to make scorched earth around the capital, and the 55 Squadron played its part with the attack by six Baltimore aircraft of the road just south of Rome between Arce and Valmontone on the night of the 9th and 10th.

Operation Strangle ended on May 11 and was undoubtedly a great success, a few days later, on May 19, all of Cassino was already in Allied hands. In the operations conducted by the 15th Air Force during Strangle, heavy bombers dropped more than 5,000 tons of bombs on the communication routes. From March 19 to May 11, MAAF operations against the lines of communication and ports, totaled about 50,000 sorties, with a total of about 26,000 tons of bombs dropped.

During the night of May 12, an armed reconnaissance saw six Baltimores of the 55 Squadron, intercept and attack German troops between the towns of Avezzano, Rieti, Terni, Spoleto and Foligno. For the night operations there was the collaboration with the Bostons of the 18 Squadron RAF, which carried out mainly tasks of illuminators for the targets, through the use of phosphorous devices. In detail, on the night between the 16th and 17th of May, in two different missions, the first between Valmontone and Frosinone, eight Baltimores of the 55 Squadron were assisted in the illumination of targets by the Bostons of 18 Squadron. The same thing happened for the attack on the port facilities between Ancona and San Benedetto del Tronto. But a bold note in the Squadron's diary reported that on that day "The Gustav Line has been destroyed".

In the month of April 1944 General Clark, strongly shaken after the repeated failures, had secretly returned to the United States where he remained for two weeks; the American leaders illustrated to the General the planned Allied planning, the so-called Operation Overlord, the great landing in France, scheduled for June 5th. They underlined, also, that it would have been propagandistically important that before that date the American troops had succeeded in liberating Rome. Clark, still determined to conquer Rome out of personal ambition, returned to Italy determined to launch a new offensive. At the same time, Winston Churchill and Alexander, were also intent on resuming operations against the Gustav Line, code-named Operation Diadem.

After the breakthrough of the sector of Cassino and in the sector of the Anzio and Nettuno landing head, the German commander Kesselring put in place a retreat of his forces on the Gothic Line so abandoning Rome.

The capital was finally liberated on 4 June 1944 by the American 5th Army, coming from the Tyrrhenian sector. The 55 Squadron did not carry out any missions that day, but the indelible pen of Wing Commander L. E. Leon marked in the Squadron's diary "ROME fell, American troops entered the city at 0.80[08:00] hours".

On the 28th of June, Wing Commander L. E. Leon allowed all personnel of the 55 Squadron, which in the meantime had moved to the Tarquinia airstrip, to visit Rome. At 07:30 a.m., a long caravan of trucks on which the personnel of the Squadron were crammed, left for Rome. They would return at 18:00, having finally set foot in Rome, admiring it and taking photographs as tourists usually do today.

At the end of 1944 Spurr returned to Egypt, but his 55 Squadron continued to carry out operations over Italy until the end of the war as part of Tactical Air Force, of which it had always been a part, along with the 232 Wing.

▲ In the distance the white silhouette of a hospital ship, heading towards the port of Vibo Marina in Calabria.

▼ The city of Termoli, along the Adriatic coast, photographed from above.

▲ Spurr and the Squadron during their entry into Corigliano Calabro, along the SS 106 Ionica.

▲ The Squadron's journey across the boot, through the winding and narrow communications routes of Calabria, which often forced maneuvers to the limit of the possible.

▼ In Spurr's few notes this photo is attributed to San Vito dei Normanni.

▲ The monument to the "Marinaio d'Italia" (Italian sailor), built during the Fascist period, is a structure in the shape of a rudder about 53 meters high that stands out on the port of Brindisi; the structure is in reinforced concrete, entirely covered in carparo (a compact calcarenitic stone of golden color). It is colloquially known among the residents of Brindisi as "la jatta 'ssittata". After the fall of the fascist regime, the fasces were removed.

▲ Workers removing the fascist symbols.

▲ The train station in Taranto, still half destroyed after the intense American bombing, including that of the B-24 Liberator of the 9th Air Force on May 4, 1943.

▼ The Petruzzelli Theater in Bari.

▲ The port of Bari. The night bombardment of Bari on December 2, 1943 was a spectacular action carried out at low altitude by Luftwaffe aircraft, with the aim of attacking the transport ships of an important convoy located inside the port, and which had been reported in the morning by German air reconnaissance.

▼ Baltimore formations of the 232 Wing RAF head for the target.

▲ Column of Sant'Oronzo in Ostuni (BR).

▼ Port of Brindisi, in the background the Federico Barbarossa Castle. In the foreground the two school ships of the Regia Marina, "Amerigo Vespucci" and "Cristoforo Colombo". The Amerigo Vespucci is still the Italian Navy's most envied school ship in the world.

▲ The Cathedral of St. Peter the Apostle, one of the largest sacred buildings in southern Italy.

▼ Striking shot from the underside of the wing of a B-24 Liberator that captures from a particular angle the landing of the Baltimore letter "L" in yellow Squadron. Note the pavement of the runway covered with grelle. We are probably on the Biferno runway.

▲ Probable entrance of the unit in Foggia towards the end of November. Shortly afterwards the American heavy bombers of the 15th Air Force would be installed in the airports of Apulia, in particular that of Foggia, to carry out actions on German targets in Germany and the Balkans.

▼ The caravan as it crosses the Trigno River. The waters of the river cross the municipalities on the border between Abruzzo and Molise, with the exception of the initial stretch of the river which is in the province of Isernia, and the final one.

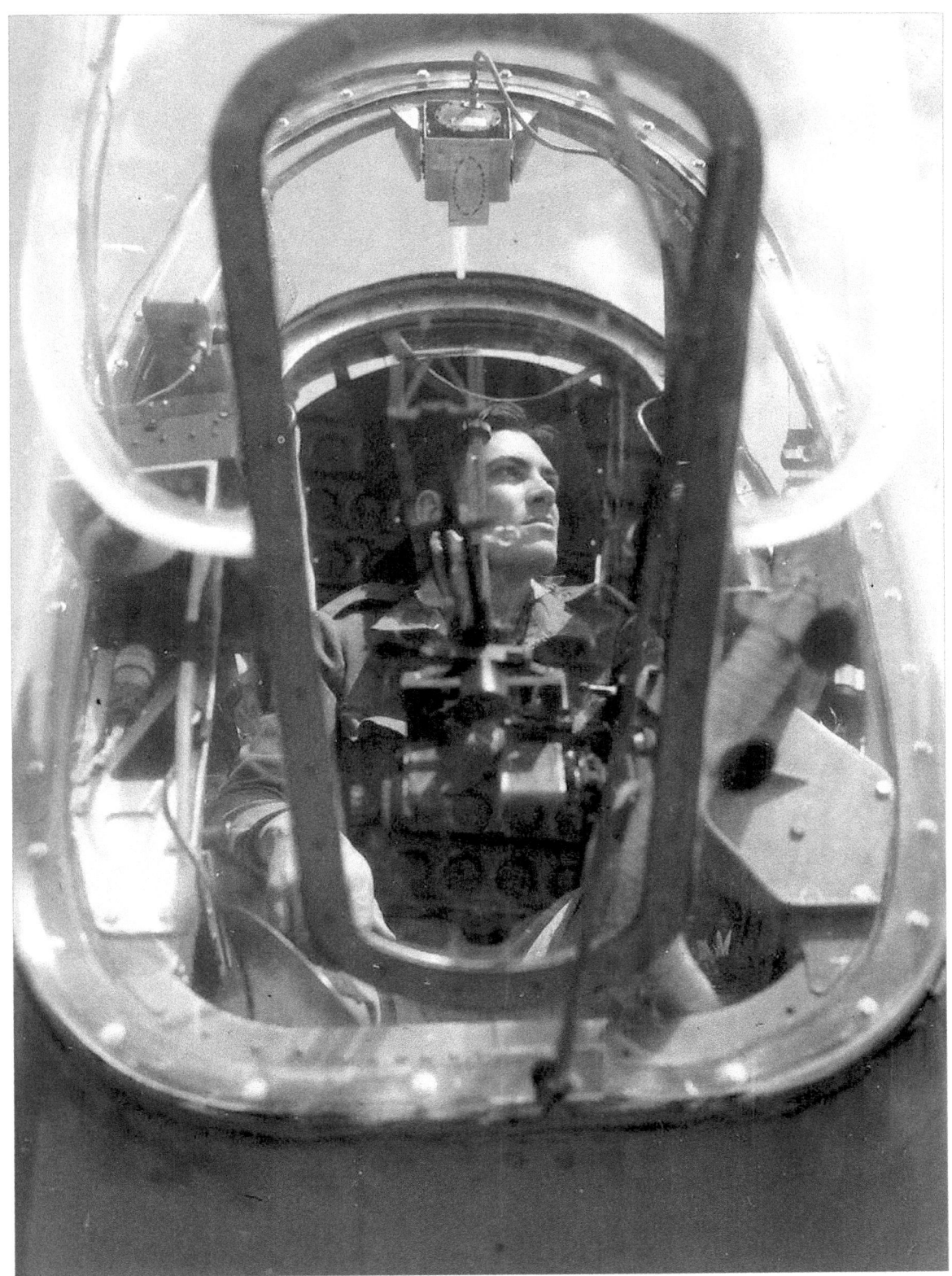
▲ Algernon de Blois Spurr inside the bow post of the Baltimore.

▲ A mixed formation of Baltimore's 232 Wing RAF and 21 Squadron SAAF attacks the town of Valmontone. The bombing was carried out shortly before 10 am.

▲ After a brief stint in North Africa, 55 Squadron returned to operations from the Biferno airstrip. At 9 a.m. on 8 April 1944, a Baltimore formation led by Wing Commander L.E. Leon DFC attacked the Rieti airfield hitting the hangars and the workshops. After this raid the enemy forces permanently ceased their activity from this airport.

▲ A Savoia-Marchetti S.M.79, with the insignia of co-belligerent Italy just landed on an Allied runway. A similar aircraft was the protagonist of the Italian surrender, transporting several times the Italian delegation to Sicily during the surrender negotiations with the Allies.

▼ The SIAI-Marchetti S.M.79 "Sparviero" was a three-engine low-wing multi-role aircraft. It was also used by the Italian Legionary Aviation during the civil war in Spain.

▲ Algernon de Blois Spurr was not just a photographer. During his time around Italy he delighted in creating pencil drawings in which he depicted the locations he passed through or simply scenes of daily life in the department.

▼ Drawing depicting the ground personnel of the department in some anti-aircraft positions defending an airfield.

▲ A Baltimore from the Squadron has just carried out the bombing of a bridge.

▲ Baltimore in flight over the alps. In 1945 the Squadron bombed locations such as Treviso, Porto Gruaro and Montebelluna, and other tactical targets in northeastern Italy.

▼ A B-26 Marauder from 21 SAAF Squadron moving away from the newly bombed target near the Adriatic coast of Italy. Starting in July 1944, this Squadron began receiving a number of B-26 Marauders.

▲ Ground and flight personnel posing in front of the Baltimore V FW390 'K'. Imprinted only on one side of the aircraft are the more than 100 bombing missions flown. The signatures of R. S. Grey and R. Davison.

▼ A SAAF B-26 Marauder, probably from 21 Squadron, is leaving the target just bombed near Pescara.

▲ A SAAF B-26 Marauder prepares for take off by taxiing on the girders.
▼ The Baltimore in flight.

▲ Art work of an air base.

▼ Another painting made by Algernon. His artistic expertise is evident!

▲ Performance at an Allied airport by Florence Dawson, better known by her stage name Florence Desmond, an English actress, comedian, and impersonator. Performance held probably between April 13 and 14, 1944.

▼ The thanks of the artists at the end of the show.

▲ Visit to Cape Marino by Jan Christiaan Smuts, a South African philosopher, soldier and politician who on two occasions was Prime Minister of the South African Union from 1919 to 1924 and from 1939 to 1948.

▼ The Tower of Pisa in an evocative flyover by a Baltimore of the 55 Squadron, whose shadow is entirely transposed to the side of the tower.

▲ The city of Pisa was attacked for the first time by the Americans on 31 August 1943. On that occasion as many as 152 B-17 flying fortresses belonging to the NASAF targeted the railway infrastructure. In the raid, also part of the inhabited center suffered damages, but the monumental complex of the tower was spared. There were hundreds of civilian casualties.

▼ The center of Pisa photographed from above.

▲ A SAAF Baltimore bogged down probably at Capodichino Airport, Naples. Ground and flight personnel without the aid of mechanical means pull the aircraft out of the quagmire.

▼ The effort of many soldiers was needed to complete the task.

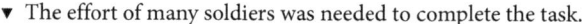

▲ One of the bombing of Pisa by American bombers. Indicated by an arrow and placed within a circle, the Tower of Pisa is clearly visible. (NARA)

▲ A long line of people, mostly military personnel on leave, cross Via della Conciliazione on their way to the Vatican.

BRIEF HISTORY OF THE 55 SQUADRON RAF

The 55 Squadron was established at Castle Bromwich on 27 April 1916 as a training unit and became the first unit to be equipped with DH4 aircraft in January 1917. In March it moved to France with bombing and reconnaissance duties, attacking enemy airfields, communications routes and bases behind the Western Front. With the formation of the Independent Force in June 1918, the Squadron was attached to 41 Wing to carry out strategic raids on German targets. After a brief period of wartime activity, it was responsible for transporting mail to the occupation forces, the Squadron was then organically downsized in January 1919 when it returned to the UK and finally disbanded on 22 January 1920.

On 1 February 1920, 142 Squadron based in Suez was renumbered as 55 Squadron and operated with DH9 aircraft, which were soon replaced by DH9As and moved to Turkey in July as part of Q Force. In September, it redeployed to air bases in Iraq. In February 1930, it was re-equipped with Westland Wapiti and then in February 1937 received Vickers Vincent. For nineteen years, the Squadron was part of the peacekeeping force in Iraq, taking part in various operations. In March 1939 the first Blenheims began to arrive and in August it moved to Egypt as war approached.

With the entry of Italy into the war in June 1940 began a series of bombing raids on airports, ports and enemy bases in Libya that continued for over a year. By March 1941, the 55 Squadron remained the only air unit equipped with daylight bombers in the entire Western Desert, the other units having moved to Greece. After a period of rest and training, the Squadron resumed operations on 12 September 1941, carrying out operations against shipping until its withdrawal to Egypt in March 1942. In May it converted to Baltimore bombers, on which it first carried out missions on 2 July. After the defeat of the Afrika Korps at El Alamein in October, the Squadron began to advance to keep within range of the enemy until it reached Tunisia, where it attacked enemy bases and airfields until the Axis forces surrendered.

From the bases in Tunisia, attacks began on Sicily in preparation for the Allied landings in July 1943, and once more airfields were ready the Squadron moved there in August. The capture of bases in southern Italy led to a further breakthrough in late September and for the remainder of the war the Squadron was engaged in attacking enemy communications routes and tactical objectives in support of the Allied armies in Italy.

In September 1945, the Squadron moved to Greece where, in June 1946, began the conversion to Mosquito until its dissolution on November 1, 1946.

On 1 September 1960, it reformed at Honington, as the Victor unit of the V-Bomber Force. In May 1965, it became an airborne refueling unit at Marham and provided tanker aircraft for long-range movements by RAF aircraft.

Bases of the the 55 Squadron in the Second World War

Fuka	11 June 1940	L. G. 98	16 July 1942
L.G. 79	10 January 1941	L. G. 86	28 August 1942
Amseat	16 January 1941	El Sirtan	7 March 1943
Bu Amud	4 February 1941	Marsa Gardane	13 March 1943
Heliopolis	15 February 1941	Medenine Main	4 April 1943
Maraua	10 March 1941	La Fauconnerie South	15 April 1943
Derna	4 April 1941	Enfidaville	1 June 1943
Gazala North	6 April 1941	Reyville	21 June 1943
Great Gambut	6 April 1941	Gela West	9 August 1943
Maaten Bagush	9 April 1941	Gerbini 3/ Sigonella	22 August 1943
L. G. 95	2 May 1941	Brindisi	27 Sept. 1943
Helwan	2 June 1941	Foggia 1/Celone	28 Oct. 1943
L. G. 100 Wadi Natrum	1 July 1941	Kabrit	4 January 1944
Aqir	9 August 1941	Biferno/Campo Marino	24 March 1944
Fuka	21 September 1941	San Severo	2 May 1944
Bu Amud	8 January 1942	Tarquinia	23 June 1944
Benina	12 January 1942	Cecina	18 July 1944
Berka Main	20 January 1942	Perugia	18 October 1944
El Gubbi	26 January 1942	Ancona(HQ)	25 October 1944
Gambut	31 January 1942	Marcianise	29 October 1944
Fuka	3 February 1942	Porto Potenza(HQ)	2 Nov. 1944
Helwan	25 March 1942	Falconara	10 Dec. 1944
Luxor	3 April 1942	Forlì	7 March 1945
L. G. 99 Amriya	10 May 1942	Aviano	12 May 1945
Ismailia	1 July 1942		

▲ On June 28, 1944 Spurr entered Rome with his fellow soldiers. A banner hung on Corso Vittorio Emanuele II reads "Welcome to the Liberators. The Democratic Union".

▼ Altare della Patria in Rome.

▲ Castel Sant'Angelo.

▼ Military trucks and lorries drive along Piazza del Colosseo.

▲ An interior view of the Colosseum, obtained by pasting and superimposing three different shots.

▼ The Vatican.

▲ The interior of Saint Peter's Cathedral.

▲ Altar of the Fatherland seen from the perspective of Via S. Marco.

▼ Gathering of a small military garrison in front of Palazzo Venezia.

▲ The arrival of the DC3 at Cecina airport with King George VI and General Harold Alexander on board, welcomed on the ground by General Mark Clark.

▼ The three on an American truck visited the departments. In the foreground the Commanding Officer of 232 Wing RAF, Wing Commander Jack F. Raulston.

▲ The map of Italy with the route of the journey that led the unit around Italy and then to Rome. All the movements made by 55 Squadron by land, sea and air are also plotted in different colors.

▲ In late October and early November, Spurr's camera captured some people engaged in the usual olive harvest.

▼ The only photo of the entire Spurr family. Brian, Algy, Wendy and Mal.

BIBLIOGRAPHY

Books
- Brookes Andrew, Air war over Italy, London, Ian Allan, 2000.
- Craven Wesley Frank, Cate James Lea, The Army Air Force in World War II vol.II, Chicago, University of Chicago Press, 1965.
- Craven Wesley Frank, Cate James Lea, The Army Air Force in World War II vol.III, Chicago, University of Chicago Press, 1965.
- De Simone Cesare, Venti Angeli sopra Roma, Milano, Mursia, 1993.
- Duma Antonio, Quelli del cavallino rampante, Roma, Edizioni dell'Ateneo, 1981.
- D'Este Carlo, 1943. Lo sbarco in Sicilia, Milano, Mondadori, 1990.
- Fagone Salvo, Ricognitori su Husky. Il ruolo cruciale della ricognizione aerea e dell'Intelligence Ultra sulla Sicilia e sul Mediterraneo. 1940-1943, Youcanprint, 2020.
- Freeman Roger A., Osborne David, The B-17 Flying Fortress Story, London, Arms & Armour Press, 1998.
- Gillies Peter S., Major, Sicily. Analysis of a combined operations battle, Air Command and Staff College Air University Maxwell, USA, 1984.
- Goss Chris, Heinkel He 111: The Early Years - Fall of France, Battle of Britain and the Blitz, Barnsley, Frontline Books, 2016.
- Granfield Alun, Bombers over Sand and Snow: 205 Group RAF in World War II, Barnsley, Pen & Sword, 2012.
- Halley James J., Squadrons of the Royal Air Force, UK, Air Britain Historians Ltd, 1985.
- Hamilton Nigel, Monty: Master of the Battlefield, 1942-1944, Milano, McGraw-Hill, 1984.
- Hammel Eric, Air War Europa. America's air war against Germany in Europe and North Africa. Chronology 1942-1945, California, Pacifica Press, 1994.
- Molony C. J. C., The Mediterranean and Middle East Volume V: The Campaign in Sicily 1943 and the campaign in Italy 3rd September 1943 to 31st March 1944, London, H.M.S.O, 1973.
- Patricelli Marco, L'Italia sotto le bombe, Roma, Laterza editori, 2007.
- Pedriali Ferdinando, L'Italia nella guerra aerea - Da El Alamein alle spiagge della Sicilia, Roma, Aeronautica Militare, Ufficio storico, 2010.
- Pedriali Ferdinando, L'Italia nella guerra aerea – Dalla difesa della Sicilia all'8 September, Roma, Aeronautica Militare, Ufficio storico, 2014.
- Plumari Angelo, Operazione Husky. La Guerra nell'entroterra ennese, Regalbuto (EN), Euno Edizioni, 2019.
- Reale S., Iacono G., Tre giorni vissuti da Eroi. Le voci dei protagonisti. Gela 10-12 July 1943, Amazon, 2020.
- Roosevelt Churchill, Carteggio segreto di guerra, Mondadori Editore, Milano 1977.
- Rust Kenn C., Twelfh Air Force story in World War II, Londra, Hersant, 1967.
- Santoni Alberto, Mattesini Francesco, La partecipazione tedesca alla guerra aeronavale nel Mediterraneo (1940-1945), Parma, Albertelli edizioni speciali, 2005.

- Shores Christopher, Massimello Giovanni, A History of the Mediterranean Air War, 1940-1945 Volume 4: Sicily and Italy to the fall of Rome 14 May, 1943 - 5 June, 1944, London, Grub Street Publishing, 2018.
- Zangrandi Ruggero, 1943: l'8 September, Feltrinelli editore, Milano, 1967.

Documents consulted at The National Archives in London

Royal Air Force operations record books:
- Serie AIR-27-518
- Serie AIR-27-523
- Serie AIR-27-524
- Serie AIR-27-519
- Serie AIR-27-1375
- Serie AIR-27-270

▲ Bombing of an unknown location.

TITLES ALREADY PUBLISHING

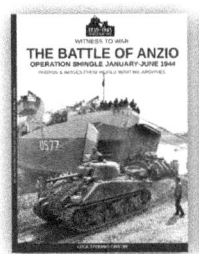

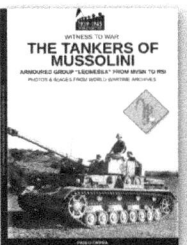

BOOKS TO COLLECT

www.ingramcontent.com/pod-product-compliance
Ingram Content Group UK Ltd.
Pitfield, Milton Keynes, MK11 3LW, UK
UKHW050411240426
12048UKWH00020B/1462